# Planning
# Your
# Retirement

# Planning Your Retirement

## The Complete Canadian

## Self-Help Guide

Blossom T. Wigdor, Ph.D.
Editor

Grosvenor House Press Inc.
Toronto~Montreal

The publishers wish to express their gratitude to
The Standard Life Assurance Company for an education
grant which helped to make this publication possible in
both English and French.

*Canadian Cataloguing in Publication Data*
Main entry under title:

Planning your retirement: the complete Canadian
self-help guide

Bibliography: p.
Includes index
ISBN 0-919959-18-0

1. Retirement — Canada — Addresses, essays,
lectures.   I. Wigdor, Blossom T., date.

HQ1062.P58 1985    646.7'9    C85-098214-6

Published by
Grosvenor House Press Inc., Toronto/Montreal
75 Sherbourne St.
Toronto, Ontario
M5A 2P9

Éditions Grosvenor Inc.
1456 rue Sherbrooke ouest
Montréal, Québec
H3G 1K4

Printed and bound in Canada

# TABLE OF CONTENTS

# Acknowledgements

I would like to take this opportunity to thank Ian Burgham of Grosvenor House Press for his patience and help in the process of developing this book and for bringing it to fruition. I would also like to acknowledge all the contributors, and editorial writers Beverley Endersby, Larry Morse and Colleen Dimson, whose skills were indispensable in producing the final product. My thanks as well to the Standard Life Assurance Company for its generous financial support of this project and for its practical editorial advice. Furthermore, this book would have been impossible had it not been for what we learned from the participants and lecturers in the various retirement seminars. We hereby acknowledge our gratitude to them and to Mr. Allan Upshall, a member of the Senior Alumini of the University of Toronto who serves as our volunteer chairman. Finally, my thanks to Margaret Klausen, Audrey Goba and Kate Hamilton for their typing of the manuscripts.

*Blossom T. Wigdor*, Ph.D.
Director, Programme in Gerontology
University of Toronto

# Preface

The longer life span of the present global population has sparked interest and concern over a relatively new phenomenon—retirement! Is it a right, a privilege, a blessing or curse, or a little bit of each? This period of later life has now resulted in an explosion of "how to" books dealing with retirement. Many of these books which have tried to cover all aspects of retirement tend to deal superficially with the topic or deal only with the author's bias or own field of expertise. There has been a need for a good resource book for the general reader covering the various aspects of retirement.

The format of this book was chosen to conform to the experience of the editor in developing retirement planning seminars for the private and public sectors including the on-going faculty and staff seminars at the University of Toronto. These seminars have been evaluated highly by the participants since their inception in 1982. The book has been authored by a number of contributors since no one person could be an expert in the various fields covered. All the contributors are recognized experts in their area and bring the best and most reliable information to the reader in the fields which are important in the preparation for retirement. This feature makes this book an important resource for individuals leading pre-retirement seminars as well as for participants in such courses. The appendix provides a separate chapter which will also be useful to such course developers and leaders. Information sources for seniors across Canada are also listed in the Appendix.

This book has been written for people who thoughtfully consider their lives, plan their futures and set goals for themselves. It is also intended for those who, faced with retirement, have questions about the factors they should consider and prepare for, or who feel some anxiety about the process of retirement and the retirement period. Thoughtful planning based on good information should make the later years an exciting and invigorating challenge.

*April 1985*

# Introduction

Many changes have been introduced into our lives during the twentieth century, so many, in fact, that it is almost incomprehensible to think that there have been more changes in the past 80 years than in the previous 2000! We are so busy trying to cope with the effects of changes upon our daily lives that we rarely take the time to assess their impact on our futures. For example, although we are dimly aware that this century's improved standards of living and health care have already extended the number of years Canadians will live, many of us have not considered the implications of that fact.

Do you remember these lines from a Beatles song: "Will you still need me/Will you still feed me/When I'm 64"? How about at 74? or 84? or 94? Did you know that when the last of the baby boomers reach the age of 65 there will be six million senior citizens in Canada? Who is going to feed them? Will there be adequate pension funds to take care of them for the 20 to 30 years of retirement facing them? Will those years be a time of joy and productivity? Or will they be years of depression and fear caused by financial insecurity? There is no doubt that if both social and economic disaster are to be averted, planning for retirement must begin *now*.

That's where this book comes in. It has been written as a comprehensive guide for those who should plan ahead for the retirement years—and it's never too early for anyone to begin. If you're in the 30s age bracket, the chapters on financial planning can show you how to get a headstart on building a retirement income. For the 40-65 age group, there are chapters on the more immediate concerns facing you such as living arrangements, estate planning to save taxes, and a host of other subjects crucial to a satisfying retirement. For the 65-plus age group, there is information on services available to senior citizens and frank answers to possibly embarrassing worries about health and finances during old age. Although financial planning is a key factor in planning a successful retirement, there are other areas of equal importance which must be considered. An understanding of the psychological and lifestyle factors which contribute to well-being is also essential. This book addresses all of these concerns and more.

## WHAT IS OLD AGE?

At one time "old age" was considered to be the period of years after retirement. Since 65 was made the mandatory retirement age in a large part of the labour market, that particular year became the indicator of old age. The 65-plus group were thus labelled "senior citizens", "the elderly", etc.

In reality, however, individuals age in very different ways and at very different rates. We all know old 50-year-olds and young 80-year-olds and more and more individuals who remain relatively healthy, involved and productive as they advance in years. Although there is still a tendency to retire at about the age of 65, if "old age" is defined as the time of life when we must give up some of our autonomy and become more dependent on others, it tends to be a very advanced age for most people— probably 85 years or more.

## THE CHANGING AGE STRUCTURE

In Canada the 65-plus age group is the fastest growing segment of the population. In 1981, 9.7 per cent of Canadians were over the age of 65. By the year 2030 it has been predicted that this segment of the population will have nearly doubled due to better control of infectious diseases and occupational hazards, a higher standard of living, healthier diets and advanced medical technology.

It is not only the increased longevity of its citizens, however, that is changing the age structure of Canada. Just as important is the country's low birth rate which has many future implications. For example, the low birth rate could cause a labour shortage by the end of the century, thus creating pressure for many older individuals to stay in the workplace. The public pension scheme could also be hard pressed to meet the needs of a proportionately larger percentage of older people, and health and social services could be stretched beyond their capacity to support all older citizens.

Most importantly, it might also mean that individuals will have to take more responsibility for their own welfare during retirement and plan more realistically than at present for that period in their lives.

## CHANGING RETIREMENT CONCEPTS

Once seen as a privilege awarded for years of hard work, retirement is now regarded as a right, as most people have contributed part of their earnings towards their post-retirement income. For many women workers, though, these contributions will not be sufficient to provide for their future needs. Because they have been in and out of the workforce due to the demands of child-raising and marriage, are often in low-paying and part-time jobs, or in service positions not covered by pension plans, their working years have not provided them with sufficient retirement funds. Dependent on spouses' pension plans which often do not have survivor's benefits, or solely on government plans, women who are now middle-aged or older have little provision for maintenance in their retirement years. In 1983, as many as 66 per cent of elderly women were receiving only government pensions and, if they were living alone in urban areas, had a cash income at or below the poverty level established by Statistics Canada.

Since women, on average, tend to outlive men by approximately eight years, planning for old age and retirement has obviously become very much a woman's concern.

There has also been a tendency to assume that the world, like Noah's Ark, is populated by couples. Recent changes in society have made this assumption no longer true as divorce and the growing choice of many people to remain single, mean that more individuals face retirement alone with resulting psychological and financial impact. Retirees falling into these categories will probably need advice about ways to counteract the problem of loneliness in their old age. This problem, along with others facing the single retiree, will be dealt with in this book.

## THE CHALLENGE OF RETIREMENT

Canadian society has well-established rites of passage for the different stages in our lives such as entering school, gaining diplomas, getting married and having children. In terms of our working lives, rewards such as titles and raises in income are bestowed upon us as we take on new and challenging careers. We are used to making plans for these different stages and we usually have some ideas about both the pleasures and responsibilities that we will experience during these different periods of our lives.

When it comes to retirement, however, although it may be marked by a rite of passage such as a farewell dinner or party, our expectations of the years lying ahead are often vague. We are left to cope with a long period of time which has few generally prescribed goals or expectations of behaviour. As well, very few of us realize that retirement is not just the act of retiring from our previous full-time occupation but a continuous process with different stages and adjustments to be made over the years. The process can also be a very different one for each individual, depending on his or her previous social, marital and economic status, as well as ability to adapt to different life experiences.

In order for an individual to plan ahead for the retirement years, it is necessary to realize *what the choices are* that lie ahead and *how these choices* can be implemented.

This book has been written in the hope that with more understanding and planning for both the needs and pleasures of the retirement years, they can become among the happiest and most productive years of your life.

# CHAPTER 1

# Planning for Change: Psychological Aspects of Retirement

*Old age is the most unexpected
of all things that happens
to a man.*

Trotsky
*Diary in Exile*

Change is perhaps the most important aspect of retirement, and adapting to change, one of the greatest challenges. The move from work to retirement can be a difficult transition. If we approach this period negatively, we could feel considerable stress and unhappiness; if approached positively, it can be an opportunity to enter a new and productive phase of personal fulfillment. In fact, studies have shown that, after a period of adjustment, a large majority of retirees report they are enjoying a high level of personal satisfaction in retirement.

Planning is the key to a successful retirement. Because most people feel that the period of retirement is too remote to consider very actively, few people plan very far ahead, and those who do make plans often wait until fairly late in life to do so. However, it is really never too early to start planning for retirement, especially in such areas as personal finances (in order to have an adequate retirement income) and good health habits (in order to be well enough to enjoy one's retirement). In other areas, such as one's personal plans for retirement, it is unrealistic to expect individuals to think about alternatives much before the age of 50 or 55. Still, even here, planning is important. Adaptation to change is an active process, not a passive one, and anticipating the changes that will occur in retirement is one of the most effective methods of coping with those changes.

## THE PSYCHOLOGICAL EFFECTS OF LEAVING WORK

Obviously the single biggest change that occurs upon retirement is the move from a period of life that is work-oriented to one that is not. Much more is involved, however, than simply working or not working. Besides providing a source of income, work has a number of other functions in our society. It can be the source of an individual's identity, it can provide social contacts, and it can serve to structure time. While the significance of these factors will vary with each individual, it is important to recognize that they all involve changes that can affect the transition from work to retirement, and the adaptations that must be made.

### Identity and Self-Esteem During Retirement

Work gives many people their identity, the way they define who they are. Work can also be a source of status for them and, therefore, a source of self-esteem. If you are this type of person, it is natural then that the loss of work that comes with retirement could result in a loss of identity and a reduced sense of personal worth. It is therefore important for you to take time to consider whether it is *only* work that is absolutely important to your identity, or if there are other aspects of your life that contribute to a sense of identity, status and self-esteem.

In retirement, we have to learn how to turn from looking for external evidence of success (praise from an employer, a raise, etc.), to taking satisfaction from the knowledge of our own past achievements and contributions. Self-esteem then becomes more of an internal matter, a question of feeling comfortable with both what we have done and with what we are presently doing. For those who still require something more, external gratification can be achieved by becoming involved in activities such as a part-time job or volunteer or community work where there's the possibility of some reward.

## Social Contacts in Retirement

For many people work is their major source of social contacts. However, once an individual leaves his or her job, there may be difficulty maintaining those relationships. This may occur because reduced contact has also reduced the interests held in common with former colleagues, or because the retiree has developed a new set of priorities. Either way, it has been found that the social ties based in the work place generally tend to be severed when one leaves. This seems to be somewhat less true for women, who tend to develop friendships that involve a greater degree of confidentiality and intimacy, whereas men's friendships tend to be more related to tasks and shared activities.

If your network of social relationships is likely to be reduced upon retirement, then part of your planning process for retirement should be to build up a network of non-work relationships to replace or substitute for the friendships that could disappear. This could be accomplished by joining organizations, participating in activities in which one already has some interest, or by exploring new areas. Some retirees have organized groups from corporations, institutions, unions, etc. which allow people with similar occupational backgrounds to continue to meet periodically. These groups tend to work well for some retirees who welcome a sense of continuity in social contacts and an opportunity to maintain their working life activities. (See chapter 2, "New Tricks: Lifestyle in Retirement" for more suggestions on ways to expand your social contacts.)

## Structuring Your Time in Retirement

Work also serves the function of providing a structure for the use of our time. While it can seem onerous and distasteful to have an external structure imposed upon one — thereby reducing opportunities for personal choice — many people, in fact, have great difficulty in using time meaningfully when such a structure no longer exists. In a structured work situation, your leisure activities usually fill the need for relaxation, rest and recuperation, or excitement, but in retirement these same activities may no longer seem so satisfying. It is, therefore, important for a retiree to develop some concept about the structure of time, and the ways he or she will want to allocate time. There is, of course, no right or wrong way to do this; where one person might like to have a planned activity to do at the same time each day, another might be happier with a schedule that changes from day to day. Your goal should be to use time in ways that are personally satisfying, and not to stay busy simply for the sake of being busy.

If there are problems with the way you are structuring your time, it might be useful to prepare a timetable. Block out the time that is needed for necessary activities, such as household maintenance. Then slot in the time that is devoted on a regular basis to ongoing interests like hobbies, recreational activities or volunteer work. The third category could then be disposable time — open time for unexpected opportunities or for activities that vary from day to day. This timetable will make the way you use time very clear; while not in itself a solution, it can serve as a basis for reallocating time in a way that will provide greater satisfaction.

## Coping with Loss and Grief in Retirement

As you grow older, the probability exists that you will experience some personal losses of either your family or friends. These losses usually involve a normal grieving period in which the loss is shared with others, who in turn provide support. Eventually, with the help of the support network, the loss is replaced with meaningful activities or relationships. It is not implied that one replaces a loss with the *same* thing, but that it is important that new things and people be sought to fulfill at least some of the important needs that the earlier relationship provided.

In just the same way, it is important for you to recognize that the loss of work, identity, income, and other changes that come with retirement can also result in a grieving period. If you realize the possibility of such reactions, you can then more readily attempt to resolve your feelings for them. You might not necessarily duplicate the work situation, but through volunteer and part-time work or other interests, it is possible to find the same kinds of satisfactions that work provided.

# GROWING OLDER

Retirement frequently compels us to confront one of the greatest changes of all—that of aging. The ability to understand aging, and to accept it as a normal part of life, is perhaps one of the first challenges that must be met in retirement. We live in a society that has negative attitudes about aging. It tends not to value age, or those older individuals who are no longer considered to be part of the producing/consuming society. These are clearly inappropriate attitudes, as older people can and do continue to make many important contributions, but many older people themselves may, in fact, accept such beliefs. If you feel negatively about growing older it will affect your adjustment to retirement. You must fight hard to overcome this attitude in order to maintain your sense of worth. The following section discusses society's attitudes about aging.

## Myths About Old Age

Society has a great many myths and stereotypes about aging, which, in large part, contribute to people's negative attitudes. While some of these views may be true for certain individuals, they are not necessarily valid for all older people. Thus, one of the first steps in accepting the aging process could be to examine these myths, and to sort out those based on reality and those that are not.

• It is difficult today to define old age. Most individuals are now living longer, and do not have significant disabilities until very late in life (age 80 or more). While there are certain physical and sensory changes that accompany aging (for more specifics, see the chapter on health, "Frankly, Doctor..."), many of these can either be corrected or compensated for. Thus, it is important to realize that you may have many years in retirement without significant restrictions due to health, and to plan accordingly.

• One common view is that, on the basis of chronological age alone, it is possible to predict a great deal about any individual — attitudes, outlooks, etc. The reverse, in fact, is the case, and it has been found that as a population ages, it tends to become more heterogeneous and diverse. Contrary to what may be generally thought, most older people are *not* sick, poor, lonely, or more religious than they were at an earlier age.

• The idea that people become more conservative as they grow older is probably true, but this conservatism may be based on the fact that change can involve more risk for an older person. However, the idea that older people are more rigid is probably untrue; any seeming rigidity may be the energy-saving mechanism of trying to solve new problems with old solutions. Most older people, when faced with the need for adaptation in new situations, can and do look for new solutions.

• The idea that eventually older people will become mentally incapacitated — senile — is one of the most common myths of aging. While there is a small proportion of individuals who will develop a disease known as senile dementia of the Alzheimer type or senile dementia related to atherosclerosis, the proportion is small, probably not more than five per cent of those over 65. The great majority of older people retain their mental faculties and their learning capacity throughout life. Since one's cognitive abilities are generally unaffected by age, learning is largely a matter of wanting to learn and of exposing oneself to learning. Many adults are fearful of placing themselves in new learning situations, yet those who do frequently receive great satisfaction. There is evidence that continuing to place oneself in learning situations and stimulating environments helps to keep one mentally alert. In short, people can continue to be creative and productive with age, provided they have the opportunity and desire to do so.

• It does seem to be true that there is physical slowing down with age, though the degree varies considerably from individual to individual. Furthermore, although one may be somewhat slower than previously, habituated tasks and familiar situations often compensate for this, and any slowing may be evident only in certain circumstances.

• One of the most prevalent myths about aging is that the elderly are asexual. The most recent evidence indicates that sexual needs remain throughout most of our lifespan, although illness and disability may affect the expression of these needs. Certainly the need for physical contact remains, though it will vary greatly depending upon what the lifetime pattern of interest and activity has been. Those people who have been sexually interested and active in earlier years tend to remain so in later years if they maintain relatively good health, and have, or find, suitable partners.

• Another common myth is that one becomes more tranquil with old age. In fact, there are problems and anxieties at every stage in life, including the older years. An older person may become more resigned or philosophical, and may surrender some earlier needs and ambitions, but older people are not imbued with some "rosy glow". Basically, there are few personality changes with age. For the most part, people continue to need the same things — love, affection, contact with people, reinforcement of self-esteem, the maintenance of things that are valued. In other words, if something was important earlier, it may continue to be important. Perhaps there will not be the same need for acquisition or achievement, but those needs may well be transformed into a greater need for interpersonal interaction or for finding activities that offer significant satisfactions.

## COPING WITH CHANGE IN RETIREMENT

Because retirement brings significant changes, as occurs with any major life change, there is bound to be a certain amount of anxiety and fear caused by unclear expectations of the future. Individuals who do not anticipate these changes and plan accordingly — who try to deal with their retirement by avoiding the issue — may develop feelings of helplessness in the face of a situation they cannot control. Such feelings can make it difficult to cope, and may in turn lead to more anxiety, stress and even depression.

Negative reactions to retirement are not uncommon. About 30 per cent of retirees, at least initially, have negative feelings about retirement or some difficulty adjusting to it.

This is particularly true for those who were forced to retire earlier than they anticipated, either because of health problems or because their jobs were lost through technological displacement. Most people, however, look forward to retirement and enjoy this period of their lives. Even those who started with negative feelings often find that, after the first year or so of making adjustments, they are quite satisfied, provided they have sufficient income and are in reasonably good health.

One of the best ways of coping with the anxiety that retirement can bring is through planning and preparation. A good way to start this process is by determining what you will need and want during retirement. The individuals who are able to adapt well to the different stages of life tend to be those who are able to reassess and integrate their needs at different stages. Thus, just as you should draw up a budget of anticipated income and expenses in retirement, so too should you look at your needs and the ways you have fulfilled them, and compare these with what you feel you will need and want in the future. The following are the kinds of questions you should consider:

• What is it that your work gives you? Does it provide status and identity? Do you depend on this status and identity for your sense of well-being?

• Do you enjoy work primarily for its social contacts? If so, how will you maintain those contacts, or establish new ones?

• Do you need something external to structure time, or are you able to do it for yourself?

• Examine what you do with your leisure time. Do you become restless on weekends and holidays? Do you have interests outside work? Are these interests involving and significant enough to be a source of satisfaction after retirement?

The answers to these questions will suggest some of the issues that must be dealt with for a successful retirement. As each person has different needs and wants, there is obviously no single prescription for a satisfying life in retirement. However, there are some general principles that you should keep in mind.

## The Importance of Continuity in Retirement

While some people thrive on change, there is evidence that individuals whose lives have continuity tend to be better satisfied than those without it. Because retirement can be a period of significant change, the transition can be made easier by maintaining your current lifestyle with a minimum of modification. In order to do this, financial planning will be necessary so that the change in income will not require drastic changes in your standard of living. A person does not change upon retirement; activities that provided enjoyment or satisfaction before retirement will probably continue to do so, and should be maintained or perhaps even expanded. Likewise, if there are elements of your work that are very satisfying, you might want to see how these elements could be continued in retirement, perhaps through a part-time job, consulting or volunteering.

As well as maintaining continuity, it's a good idea to approach significant changes cautiously. While retirement can be a wonderful opportunity for trying out new lifestyles, it is extremely important that you do not rush into radical moves — such as changing your housing, moving to a new community, or opening a small business. As such decisions can have far-reaching implications, it is important that they be carefully examined, either through study and fact finding, or through talking to people who have done similar things. In the case of relocating, perhaps you should spend six months in the new community before you make any irrevocable decisions. The key is to be realistic about retirement planning — taking into account the advantages and disadvantages of the proposed change, the things that might be lost as a result of the change, the resources (financial, emotional, physical, etc.) that are involved, and the way that all of these relate to your needs and wants.

## Involvement and Participation in Retirement

Whether you are continuing existing activities or exploring new avenues of expression, it is important to seek situations that allow the possibility of real involvement. What this means will be different with each person: it could be participating in an activity or studying a subject that you have been interested in but have never had the chance to explore; taking the trip you have long dreamt of; using your work skills and experience in a volunteer situation that helps other people; becoming attached to a cause or organization with some particular goal or mission; or simply being interested in what is going on in the world, keeping up to date, making new friends and contacts. However you do it, become *involved*—do not merely fill up your time with busy work, but do things from which you gain real satisfaction, genuine pleasure, or a sense of fulfillment and self-worth. Retirement is the time for doing, not what you *think* you should do, but what you *want* to do.

## Coping Strategies in Retirement

Many people who look forward to change welcome the opportunities retirement offers to go in new directions. For others, however, the changes that come with retirement can cause anxiety and stress. By way of a summary, the following are some suggestions for coping with change, and its attendant anxieties.

• Analyze the reasons for your anxiety. Once you have identified the cause, you can gain the information or develop the strategies necessary to counteract the anxiety. Pre-retirement planning courses provide an opportunity to share your concerns and help reduce anxiety as well as transfer information (see Appendix A).

• Look for ways to minimize the losses that leaving work can cause. Find activities that can substitute or compensate. Be creative in seeking opportunities that will provide satisfactions similar to those you received from work.

• Realistic planning—taking into account your needs, wants and resources—is the best way of dealing with change. The plans need not be long-term; if uncertainty is causing stress, make some immediate plans to "ease into retirement", thereby giving yourself some additional time to think more carefully about what you'd like to do.

• Shift from long-range goals to goals that are more immediately realizeable. For instance, don't plan to travel some time in the future if you can do it now.

• Keep flexible. The more open you are to new opportunities— the more options you permit yourself—the easier it will be to adjust to new situations.

• Keep your sense of humour. It's one of the best antidotes to stress.

# CHAPTER 2

# New Tricks: Lifestyle in Retirement

*Retire? Retire to what? I
already fish and play golf.*

Julius Boros,
American golf pro (1978)

A lifestyle does not just happen. The way we live, the things we do, are the result of choices and decisions. The choices that we make now will help to determine the kind of lifestyle that we will have when we are older.

There is no such thing as a single successful lifestyle in retirement. We are all individuals with different approaches to life. We do not easily change the habits and patterns of a lifetime, and circumstances, such as personal finances and health, can limit the options available to us. Still, despite possible limitations, our retirement lifestyle does require choices and should involve planning. This chapter will look at some of the issues and problems we should consider in order to plan for a successful retirement lifestyle.

## THE PROCESS OF RETIREMENT

Many people think that retirement is simply a matter of not working. They do not realize that it is a phase of life requiring continuous adaptation, a process of change that begins with anticipation of the event and goes through several post-retirement periods of adjustment. In short, retirement is not an event we deal with at a single point in time and then forget about; it is a *process* and as such requires continuous acceptance of change and continuous willingness to adapt. The following material explains some of the stages that you might go through during the retirement process. An awareness of these stages can help you to understand your current attitudes towards the changes that are (or will be) occurring. If you understand what to expect, you can use the information to serve as the basis for planning new activities.

## The Looking Ahead Period

When people reach their early sixties, they often begin to be reminded of upcoming changes in their lives. Friends ask about retirement plans; spouses plan extended trips or talk about living in another location; personnel managers meet with them to discuss pension plans. This phase of retirement is one in which workers begin to gear themselves for separation from their jobs. They may adopt a short-timer's attitude to their work, and begin to develop detailed ideas about what retirement will be like. For many, these fantasies will bear little relation to the reality of retirement. For instance, for most people, playing golf — no matter how much they enjoy it — will not fill what amounts to some 1800 additional hours of non-work time each year.

## The Honeymoon Period

Retirement is often followed by a euphoric period of "doing all the things I never had time to do." If your retirement has been planned and realistically anticipated, you will be more likely than other retirees who have not planned ahead to enter the honeymoon process. People report being busy and active during this period, which may last up to several years if the retiree has sufficient resources and the imagination to use them. And because a retiree usually feels pretty good at this time, there is little motivation to plan for the future stages of retirement. A possible exception to this is in the area of financial planning. If a person has done little financial planning up to this point, some advice or assistance may well be required. Most senior centres would probably be able to refer you to a financial counsellor who is knowledgeable about retirement and who would offer advice for free or for a reasonable fee.

## The Disenchantment Period

Unfortunately, every honeymoon has its end, and retirement begins in earnest when it no longer feels like an extended vacation. For example, a teacher who retires in June may not feel she has left permanently until September, when everyone else is back in school. The more unrealistic the retirement fantasies have been, the greater the letdown will be during this stage.

However, frustration or disappointment can provide the opportunity for making active changes. One way of dealing positively with disenchantment involves keeping a diary of activities for a full week.

---

### YOUR ACTIVITY DIARY

- Write down what you do during one-hour periods from the time you get up until the time you go to bed.

- At the end of the week, rate each activity as enjoyable/unenjoyable and necessary/unnecessary. Circle all activities rated as both unenjoyable and unnecessary.

- At the same time, make another list — a "wish list". Without assessing feasibility, make a list of all the things you can think of that you would like to do. Ask your partner to draw one up as well, so you can compare notes. Include everything, however unrealistic or inappropriate it might seem. For each entry on the list, determine if it could be easily done, done with some training or practice, or if it's impossible. Before you give up on the "impossibles", list why something is impossible and take another look. Many earlier constraints such as work, responsibilities for children, mortgage payments, etc., may no longer exist as problems.

---

This kind of appraisal is, of course, artificial, and many people do it naturally as they go along. However, if you're feeling dissatisfaction with what you're doing — if you feel like you're in a rut or stuck with boring or unpleasant activities — putting things down on paper can help to focus the problems and the possible alternatives. Some people might find it easier to do such an exercise if a friend or spouse participates.

## The Reorientation Period

During this stage, retirees begin to make a more realistic appraisal of their alternatives and may explore new avenues of involvement. For instance, after examining your activity diary, you might decide to eliminate one of the "unnecessary/unenjoyable" activities and substitute one of the "easily done" activities from the wish list. Start with substitutions that won't be too difficult; success encourages you to attempt further changes.

Whatever your approach, the reorientation stage is a crucial one in the retirement process. Choices and decisions made at this time can determine the quality of the remainder of your retirement years.

## Achieving a Stable Retirement

People with stable retirement lifestyles know their resources, their capabilities and their limitations and feel relatively comfortable with their lives and the people in their lives. "Stability" is a rather misleading label for this stage as the process of reorientation is — or should be — continuous. *You* are, of course, the best judge: if you're unhappy or bored, then it's obviously time for some reassessment, by whatever method works best for you.

No rigid timetable can be imposed on the development of the stages discussed above, and not everyone will go through all the stages. Some people refuse even to think about retirement beforehand and invest themselves heavily in their jobs right up until the day they leave work. Some retirees never leave the honeymoon stage, and happily travel the world for the next twenty years. And others are depressed and disillusioned for all of their retired lives. The different responses come in part from long-established work habits and from how you go about defining yourself in the absence of work.

## HOW PRE-RETIREMENT PATTERNS AFFECT RETIREMENT

Stanley Parker, a British gerontologist, suggests that a person's lifestyle in retirement is determined, in part, by his or her pre-retirement patterns of work and non-work. These patterns are described by Parker as *extension, opposition,* and *neutrality.* If you recognize that your own attitudes to work and leisure resemble these patterns it might help you to identify both potential retirement problems, and strategies for dealing with them.

# Are you an "Extension" Type?

In this first pattern the person's non-work activities are often similar in content to work. For example, the retired accountant who enjoys helping seniors prepare their income tax returns fits this pattern.

A person who conforms to this pattern has usually had a life centred around work. His or her friends and leisure activities are work-related, and therefore, in retirement, he or she will have few contacts or activities that are not somehow connected to the job. The following characteristics could be attributed to those who fit this pattern: the retiree describes himself/herself in terms of previous employment ("I am a mechanic"); previously worked long hours on the job or brought work home; previous leisure activities involved work interests or skills and were often solitary (a teacher who spent Saturdays in the library, a computer programmer who spent evenings working at home on the computer); before retirement, work demands came first ("I can't go skiing because I have to finish the annual report").

"Extension" types of people often feel lost in the early retirement stage and need to do some active planning; they must reorganize contacts and activities. Because work has been the central focus of their lives, they might begin by determining how their work skills could be utilized in retirement. For example, an accountant might find that his or her skills and expertise are welcome in private consulting to pre-retirement planning groups, or in providing financial planning services to retirees through a seniors' centre, or in working through the Chamber of Commerce to aid younger people who are establishing businesses. By using existing interests and skills in these ways, the retiree is likely to come into contact with many new people who are potential friends. Thus, the new work activities can lead to new personal contacts, all within a relatively familiar context.

Being unhappy in retirement is not entirely unlike being unhappy in a job; the way to deal with it can be much the same. If you are unhappy with your job, you might make a list of your marketable skills and attributes — both personal and work-related — and begin to explore ways to find a position that would offer greater satisfaction. In retirement, the same kind of assessment could help you to locate activities that are more personally meaningful. Employment agencies for retired executives, "second look" groups for women interested in new directions, and career-counselling organizations might be able to help with the process.

In a way, the "job" of retirement is to use your new leisure time in activities that are satisfying, whatever that may mean for each individual.

## Are you an "Opposition" Type?

In the second pattern, a person deliberately chooses leisure activities that are different from work. For example, workers with office jobs engage in physical activities such as carpentry during their leisure time.

In contrast to those who fit the "extension" pattern, "opposition" people often look forward to retirement since they did not really enjoy their work, and saw their jobs as a 9-to-5 means to an end. Their leisure activities were different from work and their friends were both from work and outside. In retirement, the person who fits this pattern does not see his or her identity necessarily in terms of previous employment. This type of person is likely to have the advantage of a repertoire of non-work activities and friendships with which he or she can continue after retirement.

However, some "opposition" people who anticipated retirement are surprised to experience feelings of disappointment. It is one thing to enjoy an activity as a break or rest from something that is disliked, but once the tension is removed, that same activity can become much less attractive. If disenchantment arises for this type of person, the same sort of assessment of personal and work-related skills as suggested above might be useful. The inventory in itself might suggest some new activities to explore, as this kind of person already has a history of pursuing activities that are not connected to a job. Perhaps this person will find that it helps to have some work (paid or unpaid) to balance the leisure time. If this is the case, the same organizations mentioned above (employment agencies for retired executives, etc.) might be able to provide assistance. In general, although the "opposition" person will probably start the process of reorientation later than the "extension" person, the process is just as important.

## Are you a "Neutrality" Type?

The third pattern can be seen as fitting midway between the previous two because the person who fits this pattern is not very involved in either work or non-work activities. For the "neutrality" person, work was just another part of the day's routine and neither particularly enjoyed nor disliked. This type of person probably had few active leisurely pursuits, and relatively few friends, and might describe him or herself as a shy or private person.

In one sense, people who exhibit this third pattern seem to be good candidates for retirement since work will disappear with little fanfare, and they may not have high expectations or demands for what follows. The problem here is that the "neutrality" type of person may transfer the boredom felt on the job to the whole of retired life. They are also the least likely to make plans as their approach to life is already somewhat passive. If such is the case, this person is unlikely to turn into an active planner upon retirement and may need some help in order to come up with a way to structure leisure time. One possibility for this type of person might be to join a Senior Centre which offers many activities and outings and has members who are more than willing to welcome someone new. Another might be to get in touch with a local volunteer centre: many communities have an organization which recruits volunteers for a wide range of activities, from fund-raising to tutoring a learning-disabled child.

For those who fit the third pattern, retirement can offer an opportunity to change old habits since it disrupts a comfortable routine and requires that something new be established in its place. Of course, it's necessary that there be an interest in keeping active and a willingness to take the first step. If the "neutrality" person does want to change, it is advisable for him or her to try to do so early in retirement, before inertia sets in.

## RELATIONSHIPS IN RETIREMENT

Of all the factors influencing the quality of your life in retirement, relationships will undoubtedly be one of the most important. Few of us want to live our lives in isolation, but maintaining (or developing) positive relationships with our family and friends in retirement may require some new and different strategies. Lifestyle planning in retirement includes planning for and with the people in your life; as surely as income changes after retirement, so too do the patterns of social contact. An awareness of these changes in advance can either help to keep problems from arising or make it easier to come up with strategies if they do.

## Couples and Retirement

"I married him for better or for worse but not for lunch." "Twice the husband on half the salary." "What do I do with him 24 hours a day?" Many of these clichés about retirement make it clear that spouses will have to make some adjustments. However, despite these clichés, male workers are inclined to see retirement primarily as a personal affair. Their wives may even agree, feeling that since they have never stopped working around the house, retirement is hardly an issue for them.

Couples with these attitudes could have some unpleasant surprises ahead. Whereas one partner may be in the honeymoon stage of retirement, blissfully unaware of anything but contentment, the other may be disillusioned by the disruption caused by increased togetherness. Consider the honeymoon from the point of view of the wife of a recent retiree.

Six months ago, Ruth's husband, Bill, retired after 40 years of working for a large corporation. They took a long-awaited trip to Europe and returned home in late summer. For Ruth, this was the point when coping with Bill's retirement began in earnest. Suddenly she was faced with a whole new set of decisions. Should she, as she had always done, become involved in the usual autumn activities — yoga, bridge club, church groups — that took her out of the house for several afternoons each week? Or should she give up some of her personal pursuits and develop new activities that would include Bill? How much should she expect him to share in the housework that she had always done by herself? He seemed willing to help, but she could do most things more efficiently alone. Also, her husband had seen little of his former colleagues since he retired; should she help him contact old acquaintances or encourage him to develop new ones?

Ruth saw her job as helping Bill to retire from his. Since retirement wasn't something that she was facing directly, she felt she should keep her concerns to herself. In doing so, however, she risked not truly understanding his needs as well as denying many of her own. Their situation contains a number of the key issues that husbands and wives have to confront in retirement — questions concerning togetherness, privacy, contact with former friends and colleagues, and running the household.

# Togetherness in Retirement

Wives seem more likely than their husbands to report that they must spend too much time with their spouses, and that the demands on their time have increased. Many women who have been free for years to organize their time, feel that their husband's needs predominate after his retirement. For most wives, the pleasure of the time spent with their spouse and the satisfaction of feeling needed seems to offset the loss of personal freedom. They often take charge of the planning, organizing some separate and some joint activities to moderate the amount of time spent together. A smaller group of women consider that their choices about their own activities have been resolved and resent what they see as decreased control over their own lives. For both groups, "togetherness" is seen as the wife's problem, and they often do not talk to their husbands about the adjustment they must make to his retirement.

---

## YOUR TOGETHERNESS CHART

1 For the last year you (or your spouse) were working, estimate the number of waking hours you spent together each week from Monday to Friday. What were the usual activities you did together in the morning, during the day, in the evening?

2 Estimate the number of waking hours you spent apart each week from Monday to Friday. What were the usual activities you did in the morning, during the day, in the evening?

3 Repeat 1 and 2 for the current week.

4 Compare the two lists, asking yourself the following questions: Are we spending more time together? If yes, how much time? If you could choose, would you spend more, less, or the same amount of time together? What "together" activities have you continued to do? What have you given up? Have any been added? What separate activities have you continued to do? What ones have you given up? Have any been added?

---

The question for all couples is "How much is enough?" What is excessive for one person may be fine for another. In any case,

24 hours a day together can become excessive for even the most loving couple. The preceding exercise might be useful for those of you who feel there's a little too much togetherness in the relationship.

This information can help you plan ways to deal with excessive togetherness. Some possible strategies might include reinstituting an individual activity given up since retirement or replacing it with another. You will be a more interesting partner if you do some things apart from your spouse. Or you might take an adult education course on any topic, especially one that is new to you. Remember that if you're bored, you may well be boring to be with. Negotiate your "apart" time with your spouse — Thursday evening, two afternoons a week, whatever works best for both of you. Work out "apart while together" strategies. Can you go into the den, close the door, and read a book for an hour? If you prefer to prepare dinner alone, can you encourage your spouse to read the paper, take the dog for a walk, etc.?

## Privacy in Retirement

Privacy is obviously related to the question of togetherness. For a homemaker who has always had the house to herself for several hours a day, a husband at home inevitably means a loss of privacy. For a retiree who may have worked in a busy office, being at home with only one person may seem like isolation.

There are two issues that often arise as couples work out the amount of personal space each partner requires. The first is that privacy is often measured according to what existed previously. Thus, while the retiree may look forward to activities with his spouse to alleviate his solitude, she may long to escape into a good book to increase hers. A second issue involves individual attitudes to privacy. There is an assumption that husbands and wives want to spend time together and will not require time away from one another. Also, many women, well aware that others have already lost their spouses, feel fortunate to have a husband with whom to spend time in retirement. Thus, a wife may feel she should give up the private times she had when her husband was away at his job.

The following are some of the problems relating to privacy that may arise with retirement. These may seem to be relatively small issues, but unless they are dealt with, they can grow to become major problems.

• Telephone calls. Although spouses may say (and mean) that they have no secrets, it can be difficult to get used to having someone always around who hears half of every conversation, and who wants a report on every telephone call. An extension phone in another room can be a simple solution to this problem, as well as helping to contribute to some additional "time apart".

• "Me and my shadow". What happens if you try to get some space by taking the dog for long walks and your spouse decides to come along? You can try the indirect approach — get up very early if your spouse likes to sleep in, or go when he/she is otherwise occupied. The direct approach, used gently, may also be effective: tell your spouse that you like that time to think, plan, clear the cobwebs. Most spouses, glad to have time to themselves, will take the hint.

• Being left out. The fund-raising committee is coming to your home for a meeting and your spouse is not involved. If your home is large enough, it may be easy for your spouse to do other things and not feel banished. If it is not, it is wise to talk about the event. A newly retired husband can feel like an intruder in his own home if such events are not discussed. Likewise, wives can feel resentful if they cancel events they had previously enjoyed.

As with the question of togetherness, there are no absolute rules as to how much privacy is enough. It depends upon previous patterns, similarity of interests, and the quality of the marriage. Each couple must work out their own balance. Sometimes couples find that the increased time they spend together in retirement brings into focus tensions in their marriage that were hidden during the busy times of work, raising children, and running a household. If the problems are severe, it may be a good idea to seek some outside assistance. The following are some of the options available:

• Your minister, rabbi, or priest may be trained in pastoral counselling, or be able to refer you to someone who is.

• Some Senior Centres have pastoral counselling institutes where such help is available.

• Organizations such as the Family Service Association have trained counsellors who can provide assistance.

## A CHECKLIST:
## YOUR RELATIONSHIP WITH YOUR PARTNER

Check √ the appropriate response

| | SOMETIMES | USUALLY | ALWAYS |
|---|---|---|---|
| **A** Do I listen to my partner? | ☐ | ☐ | ☐ |
| Do I understand my partner's need: | | | |
|    for independence? | ☐ | ☐ | ☐ |
|    for privacy? | ☐ | ☐ | ☐ |
|    for socializing? | ☐ | ☐ | ☐ |
|    for friends of his/her own? | ☐ | ☐ | ☐ |
|    for activities of his/her own? | ☐ | ☐ | ☐ |
|    for loving? | ☐ | ☐ | ☐ |
|    for sharing? | ☐ | ☐ | ☐ |
| Do I respect my partner's ability to continue to manage his or her leisure responsibilities? | ☐ | ☐ | ☐ |
| Do I discuss my leisure concerns with my partner? | ☐ | ☐ | ☐ |
| Do I criticize my partner's activities? | ☐ | ☐ | ☐ |
| Do I resent being criticized about my activities? | ☐ | ☐ | ☐ |
| Do we make leisure plans together? | ☐ | ☐ | ☐ |

**B** What would I like to strengthen in our relationship during increased amounts of uncommitted time?

ME_____

_____

PARTNER_____

_____

**C** What would I like to change in our relationship to improve the time spent together?

ME_____

_____

PARTNER_____

_____

• Marriage enrichment and marriage encounter groups can be very useful for people who want to renew their marriages. Some groups are church-oriented, others are not. Information can be obtained through churches or community service organizations.

• Private therapists are listed in the Yellow Pages of most telephone books. Check their qualifications before you go, and get a recommendation if possible. A good therapist will likely be a member of the American Association of Marriage and Family Therapy or the Psychological Association, or will be a social worker or a pastoral counsellor.

## Maintaining Social Contacts in Retirement

Retirees often find that the job was the main thing they had in common with co-workers, and that after retirement they are not included in office social events. In fact, one of the biggest disappointments for men in early retirement seems to be the loss of contact with former colleagues from work. Retirees will find that they must maintain or develop enough friendships so as not to feel isolated. This may be easier said than done, but the following are some strategies that might be considered:

• If the people from the office don't call, take the initiative and call them. Invite them for dinner, a drink, a movie, whatever kind of entertainment seems most appropriate. Remember, you are the one who has time to plan such things, and you want to find out which people will remain friends and which were just co-workers. If you get little response after several attempts, at least you have tried. A lack of response from former co-workers need not be taken as a personal affront. Friendships require contact and shared experiences, both of which are less common between retirees and workers.

• Take stock of your friendships. Who are the people you would call friends? Which of them have you seen lately? What are your shared interests now that you are retired? Contact at least one friend this week if you have been out of touch.

• Make a list of possible sources of new friends. If you are inter-

The checklist opposite is reproduced from *Options: A handbook of retirement information and exercises for individuals and partners shifting gears and planning their leisure in later years* (1984), with the permission of the Ontario Ministry of Tourism and Recreation, Recreation Branch.

ested in developing new friendships, you must be involved in the community. You don't meet a lot of interesting people when you are weeding the garden. But you might meet some at a garden club or a course on horticulture. If you pursue your interests in places where there are likely to be people with similar interests, chances are very good that you will make new friends.

Homemakers don't experience the same disruption in friendships and contacts at retirement. However, the homemaker needs to find ways to balance her time so that she can continue her individual friendships as well as visit the friends she shares with her husband. Couples in this situation might consider the following:

• How many of her friends are also his friends?

• Which of her activities with friends could be shared with her husband, and which could not?

• How often do they see mutual friends? Is this enough for each of them?

• Does she feel guilty when she spends time with friends without him?

• Does he resent the time she spends with friends?

These questions will help couples assess whether the balance of friendships is wrong. If it is, they might try some moderate adjustments, such as substituting an activity they do as a couple for an individual one, or entertaining a couple they have met previously but don't know very well.

## Running the Household in Retirement

This is a major issue for many couples who agree to share the household work, but then sabotage one another's efforts. She remakes the bed after he has done it; he privately admits he has no interest in learning how to cook. Men who have been used to managing people at work may take on the household management, only to be surprised at the strength of their wives' resistance. Although such experiences may provide fuel for entertaining stories at parties, resolution of these differences is crucial for harmonious retirement living. The following are some possible approaches that might be considered.

• Continue previous patterns. For some couples this means that the wife does most or all of the household activity, for others the jobs will be shared. The advantage of this strategy is that no negotiation is required. (Also, after a flurry of rearranging household tasks upon retirement, the majority of couples settle back into a division of labour that is much like that in pre-retirement.) A disadvantage is that there may be more work to do with two people at home — more meals to prepare, two sets of interests and schedules to accommodate. The woman who finds herself doing it all — in fact doing more than before — may be resentful. The homemaker must remember that her husband may not know that she is now doing more work, since he wasn't there before to see what she did.

• Increase the sharing of household tasks. This approach makes sense in that if the work is shared, either husband or wife would know how to manage on their own if necessary, and free time is increased if the work is done together. Some strategies to make it work: decide who will do what and then let him/her do it; ask for help from your spouse if you are learning a new task (assuming you want help); remember that your standards may not be the same as those of your spouse (does it really matter if the bedspread is not on straight?); new jobs can take a while to learn, so persevere; try to keep advice-giving to a minimum (he may know a lot about management, and she may have been ironing shirts for 30 years, but unsolicited directions are rarely seen as helpful).

• Decide to spend a certain amount of time on household tasks and no more. This may require a willingness to accept a lower standard of tidiness, but it can free the couple to do other things without feeling guilty.

• Hire some help if it can be afforded. A cleaning person one half-day a week can keep things tidy while the couple does other things.

## HOW TO HANDLE TWO RETIREMENTS IN ONE FAMILY

Approximately 50 per cent of Canadian women are now in the workforce. If this trend continues, an increasing percentage of couples will be faced with decisions about two retirements, which could present problems because of the different stages and timing of the husband's and wife's careers.

Women's work careers are likely to have been somewhat different from those of their husbands. Women who are now near retirement age typically married older men and left the workforce either upon marriage or upon the birth of their first child. Of those who returned to work, many did so after a lengthy absence. Thus when their husbands reach retirement age after

---

## RETIREMENT READINESS CHECKLIST

1 Will your pension and other income allow you to maintain your current standard of living?

2 Are you looking forward to retirement?

3 Have you developed concrete plans for retirement activities to take the place of work?

4 Does your spouse support your retirement plans?

5 Have you decided where to live after retirement?

6 Do you have good friends who are not co-workers?

7 Are you now engaged in activities that will help keep you physically fit after retirement?

8 Have you had a physical examination in the past year to determine whether you have any health conditions that might restrict your retirement activities?

9 Is your intake of alcohol moderate (no more than two drinks per day)?

10 Are you within ten pounds of your ideal weight?

If you answered YES to all ten questions, you are a good candidate for retirement. Six to nine YES answers indicates you have some work to do before you are ready. Fewer than six YES answers suggests that you are not yet ready for retirement.

---

thirty or more years in the workforce, wives, after only half as many years of employment, may be at the peak of their productivity and enjoying their work. By virtue of differences in age, number of years worked, and the kind of work experiences, retirement decisions will be based on different sets of factors for wives and husbands.

## Who is Ready to Retire?

Research has shown that most 65-year-olds report that they are ready to retire, particularly if they think their retirement income will be adequate to meet their needs. They cite reduced interest in their jobs, boredom, and anticipation of freer choices in retirement as reasons for this readiness. As most of these studies have been done with men, little is known about how younger women with fewer years in the workforce feel about retirement. However, findings from other studies show that workers who retire earlier than they had expected are the people most likely to feel negative about retirement. Thus, because it seems likely that partners may not share an equal interest in retirement or be ready to retire at the same time, they will need to discuss at length their readiness for retirement. The checklist opposite could serve as a starting point for such considerations.

## Who is a Better Retirement Candidate?

Some have argued that women are better candidates for retirement than men since men leave their only job upon retirement, but women retain one of two jobs — that of homemaker. In addition, women are more likely to have had some practice with retirement because of their experience of moving in and out of the workforce to raise children. However, a woman at the peak of her career may see herself as too young to retire, and she may be eligible for fewer pension benefits. Each partner in a couple will have to judge whether one or the other is likely to be a better candidate for retirement. The checklist opposite can be useful here. Additionally, couples should ask themselves the following questions:

• Is each person ready to retire?

• If only one is ready to retire, what would be the advantages/disadvantages of that person retiring and the other continuing to work?

- If the husband retires first, is he willing to take on the responsibility of household management while his wife works?

- If only one is ready to retire, what would be the advantages/disadvantages of both retiring or both continuing to work?

It might be useful for each partner to evaluate his/her patterns of work and non-work as described earlier. Extension, opposition, and neutrality patterns may be good predictors of a person's adjustment to retirement. They may also give couples a basis for identifying areas in which their preferred retirement lifestyles might differ.

A pre-retirement planning course might also prove helpful in trying to decide the issue of who should retire. The focus of the course should be broader than the financial aspects of retirement in this case. Check the course outline and the qualifications of the instructor to make sure that the material will be relevant.

## What's Your Marriage Like?

The honeymoon stage of retirement has some similarities to the original bridal honeymoon. If there were children, it may well be the first occasion since early marriage that the couple has had uninterrupted time together. However, while the intense togetherness of the first honeymoon ends when one or both of the partners returns to work, the retirement honeymoon may go on for twenty years. Some marriages are strengthened and enhanced by the opportunities provided by this. In others, it becomes apparent that children and work provided a distraction from marital tensions. Besides the reasons already presented (reduced privacy, too much togetherness, etc.) there are other ways in which retirement can heighten stress in a marriage:

- One or both members might be unhappy about retirement.

- The retiree is seen by one or both as having less status.

- The couple may have to rely more on each other in the absence of work.

- Patterns are disrupted in retirement, and the partners may resent one another because of the upset.

- Without work and children to distract them, a couple may find that they have little in common.

• If people are bored, they sometimes blame others close to them.

A couple, aware of stress (or potential stress) in their marriage, might well consider a phased retirement to allow them to develop strategies to deal with those tensions. These might include:

• Taking a marriage enrichment course.

• Getting busy with retirement activities. This will relieve boredom, reduce the amount of time spent together, give the couple something to talk about, and perhaps lead to new friendships.

• Giving it some time. All changes as major as retirement will cause some upset. It may take as long as a year to develop new patterns.

• Seeing a counsellor if tensions persist.

## FACING RETIREMENT ALONE

The changing patterns of marriage and divorce, and society's increased acceptance of the single person's status means that there will be a larger proportion of people who reach retirement without a spouse. The retirement decisions they face vary, depending upon whether they are male or female, and the length of time they have been single.

## Retirement for the Never-Married

The never-married person might be considered one of the best candidates for retirement. For the most part, his or her decisions about retirement are personal and need not be made in negotiations with other family members. Because single retirees have had to develop their own network of social contacts throughout life, they can continue in retirement to draw heavily on extra-familial social contacts. For them, retirement is more likely to be a matter of continuity than an abrupt change.

However, intimacy is important to people of all ages, and one or more close, enduring relationships can act as buffers against the upsets that often accompany retirement. Spouses often serve this role for married people, but the never-married retiree does not have the advantage of that built-in relationship.

Although never-married men are more likely than women to have a higher post-retirement income and to own their own homes, they tend, in general, to have more difficulty making and sustaining intimate friendships in retirement. Also, there are far fewer single older men than single older women, since most retired men are married and a large proportion of older women are widowed. Hence, men have fewer possibilities for friendships with men in the same situation as themselves. Some single men are also uncomfortable with what they perceive as pressure from single women looking for a new spouse, while others enjoy being in demand.

Although single women are less likely to choose early retirement because they are not in a good financial position, many are in jobs that have little security, and have to retire earlier than they would like. Women have lower average salaries than men, which means they have less discretionary income and are less likely to be able to acquire assets during their working lives. They are also more likely to be involved in jobs where there are no pension plans. For these reasons, and without a spouse's income to fall back on, single women are particularly vulnerable in retirement. Even though one of the major thrusts in pension reform is towards making pensions more equitable for women, single women must pay particular attention to financial planning in retirement.

Some single women must also consider family demands in conjunction with retirement decisions. Single daughters continue to be considered the likeliest candidates to provide care for frail, older family members — often their own parents. One of the ironies of the increased life expectancy is that we now have two generations of retirees. The very old may have a rather lengthy period of some dependency on others, while the new retirees, who might otherwise have been free to come and go as they please, are tied much more closely to home. While many people feel this is a reasonable compromise, they do have a much more limited scope in which to develop retirement activities.

## Retirement for the Widowed

The loss of a spouse has a profound impact on the lifestyle of most people. When someone loses his or her spouse around retirement, there are many more adjustments to be made, and the recently widowed are the group least likely to be satisfied with retirement, unless they have had some time to adapt to being on their own.

The experts disagree about whether retirement is more diffi-cult for the widow or the widower. Retired widows have the advantage of a potential friendship network of women in the same situation, are more likely than men to have homemaking skills, and have somewhat closer ties to their adult children. They have usually developed social skills (writing letters to friends and relatives, organizing events like birthday and anniversary parties for family and friends, taking the initiative in making social contacts) which give them a network of people to carry with them into the retirement years.

Widowed women, however, often experience a dramatic drop in their standard of living after the death of their husbands. Many may find that they are not entitled to their husband's pension, or that payments are much lower than they would have been had he survived. Besides having less money, many widowed women also find that they are lacking in money management skills. Their husbands "took care of all that", but they were not doing their wives a favour. Women who are married should find out about their financial affairs. The middle of a crisis, such as when a spouse is ill, is hardly the best time to learn about financial management. However, there are a number of ways to acquire some skills in money management:

- Take one of the many adult education courses on subjects such as income tax, investments, money management.

- Contact the provincial Department of Consumer and Corporate Affairs for pamphlets on money management.

- Some provinces, such as Alberta, New Brunswick and Nova Scotia, have Home Economics Divisions within the provincial Department of Agriculture. Each has consultants and courses in various areas of home management, includ-ing finances.

- Contact the local Senior Centre for a referral, perhaps to a retired banker or accountant, for financial assistance.

Widowers seem to have the edge in financial matters. They are likely to have higher retirement incomes than widows and more experience in money management. If they are considering remarriage, it is easier for them to find a mate than it is for a widow as there is a large group of eligible women from which to choose. If they are looking for male friends, however, there are relatively fewer men around than there are female friends for the widow. Those widowers who had traditional marriages are also less likely to have skills in cooking and household management. As is the case with women and finances, men should ask their wives to show them how to do things. The best time to learn about running a house is when you have a skilled consultant right there. If that is not possible, there are a number of other ways to deal with household management:

---

- Buy a basic cookbook. There are many on the market that give instructions for the beginner.

- Take an adult education course on cooking. It will teach skills, as well as offering an opportunity to meet new people.

- Hire someone to clean periodically if you can afford it; it will help keep you organized until you learn some of the skills.

- Ask a friend or neighbour how to go about certain tasks; most people are flattered to be asked (as long as they aren't expected to do the work).

- Many Senior Centres have skills exchanges; you may be able to fix someone's tap in exchange for some casseroles to put in the freezer.

---

## Retirement for the Divorced

It is estimated that approximately 40 per cent of Canadians will be divorced during their adult lives. Thus, increasing numbers of previously married people will be unmarried in retirement. As with widowhood, the best candidates for coping well with the transition to retirement are those who have had the longest amount of time to adjust to the divorce. Issues that the divorced face in retirement are similar to those experienced by the widowed, with possible differences in friendship networks and financial resources.

Despite the increasing incidence of divorce, many people have some difficulty deciding how to relate to the two people who used to be a couple. For the divorced person this may mean the loss of some friends who feel stronger loyalties to the ex-spouse. Unlike his or her widowed counterpart, the divorced person is likely to be subject to disapproval and may be abandoned by some acquaintances. With the additional loss of some work-related friendships, the recently divorced person may need to make the development of new friendships a high priority for retirement.

It is difficult to make more than general comments about the financial situation of divorced people in retirement. Recent property settlements have tended to favour sharing of matrimonial assets, including pensions. This means that many divorced people face retirement with minimal pensions and with a much reduced equity in the house. Women who have been divorced and remained unmarried are especially likely to have a lower retirement income. Many did not enter the workforce until after a divorce, and thus will not have as many pension credits as someone who worked longer.

The divorced who have remarried may have several additional issues to consider when planning for retirement. They may still have children to support after they themselves have retired, and may have incurred large debts, such as mortgages, much later in life than those who remain married to their original partners. Thus, people in second marriages may have more financial commitments and responsibilities upon retirement and must plan accordingly.

## FRIENDSHIPS IN RETIREMENT

One of the assumptions often made about the impact of retirement is that the retiree will be cut off from friends at work and will consequently feel isolated and lonely. Although it may be inevitable that the retiree sees fewer of his or her former colleagues, it cannot be assumed that this is necessarily upsetting. As some social contacts are imposed by the requirements of the job, one of the bonuses of retirement can be the elimination of those obligatory relationships. The work friendships retained (if any) may reflect the retiree's previous patterns. As mentioned earlier, the "opposition" person may already have a group of friends he or she met through hobbies and leisure activities, while the "extension" person may have few friends who were not former workmates and might well need to develop new relationships in retirement.

# The Patterns of Friendship

In terms of opportunities for friendship, workers have an advantage over non-workers in that most have daily contacts with a group of people with whom friendships might develop. Retirees have no such ready-made reference group unless they happen to live in a situation like a retirement community. Even so, it is not clear if those with access to a wide group of people actually have more friends than those who have contact with a smaller group; it could be far more important to have an interest and skill in developing new associations. Certainly, there will not be much opportunity for making new acquaintances if one stays home watching television.

Women have somewhat different patterns of friendship than men, and tend to have more close friends than men do. Women will also most often name another woman as their closest friend, but men usually name their wives. Thus, women are more likely to have a group of friends to provide support in times of crisis. Men who have lost their wives through death or divorce can be particularly vulnerable if they lack a group of supportive friends.

There is no indication that having a large number of friends necessarily leads to greater satisfaction in retirement. A person with a small number of friends can be just as satisfied as one with a great many friends. However, those who are happiest in retirement report having an adequate number of friends, and sufficient contact with those friends. Exactly what that means will be different for each person. The following questions might be helpful in determining the adequacy — the quality and breadth — of one's friendships:

---

## FRIENDSHIP CHECKLIST

- Is there someone I can call if I want some company to do an activity I enjoy?
- Do I have someone who is close whom I can confide in? Do I see that person often enough so that he or she knows what is going on in my life?
- Do I have at least some friendships that are "equal" — in which I don't think I am receiving more than I am able to give?
- Am I able to develop new friends when others are lost because people move away, become ill, or die?
- Do I see enough of my friends?

- Do I see too much of some friends?
- If I were to move to a new location tomorrow, who would I miss most? What aspects of that friendship give me pleasure? What could I do to try to replace it?

For those who feel they may lack some of the social skills needed to develop new friendships, the following are some suggestions for ways to deal with the problem:

- Take adult education courses in such things as communication skills, interpersonal relationships, or public speaking.

- Join an organization such as the Rotary Club where social contacts are assured through membership.

- Ask a more social friend to make introductions, and go along when invited to new activities.

While it is not always easy to replace the friendships and social contacts that may be lost with retirement, retirement also brings with it the time to develop new contacts. The following are just a few of the ways to go about this:

- Get involved in activities you enjoy. If you meet some interesting people, it's a bonus; if you don't, you still have done something you enjoy.

- Adult education. At least twice a year (September and January) most communities publish a list of the adult education courses that are available. Decide to take at least one each time. Furthermore, many universities now offer summer courses for seniors in which a wide range of non-credit interest courses are offered. Many of these programs allow the person to live on campus, use the library, and take part in specially organized social events. The registrar's office of the university would have details.

- Get involved in a political party. You'll meet like-minded people, and find out more about the political system no matter how disillusioning that might be.

## HOW TO PLAN YOUR RETIREMENT LIFESTYLE

When you are planning a retirement lifestyle, it is obvious that the fewer the limitations you have, the easier it will be to make choices and decisions. For instance:

- The person who is physically fit can choose a whole range of activities in retirement that require a fit body. If you are out of shape, a fitness program can greatly enhance stamina and flexibility.

- The person who owns a home probably has more disposable income to do other things. The person who still has a mortgage, however, can reduce housing costs by moving into less expensive accommodation, and thus increase options in other areas.

- The person who has a large group of friends has choices about which friendships to maintain in retirement. The person with fewer friends, or with friends still at work, will have to put more energy into activities that bring contact with new people.

The ideal situation would be to begin planning your retirement lifestyle several years before it happens. Still, even with no prior planning, the changes inherent in retirement encourage people to think about lifestyle. The following exercise might be useful in this regard. Imagine yourself two months after retirement:

- Where are you living?
- Who else lives there?
- What time did you go to bed last night?
- What time did you get up?
- What did you have for breakfast?
- What are you going to do today?
- Who did you see last week?
- What are you looking forward to?

If you do this exercise seriously, you can find out a great deal about both the positive and the negative aspects of your expected retirement lifestyle. The next step is to determine what has to be done to establish your desired lifestyle. For instance, if you see yourself in a condominium in Hawaii, what do you have to accomplish to achieve that goal?

This exercise may also reveal that each member in a couple has very different views of a retirement lifestyle. The following might be one way to reconcile the differences:

- Make a list of agreed-upon areas, and details of how to achieve those.

- Make a list of areas of difference. Each person should then put priorities upon these.

- Starting with the least important (and therefore the easiest to negotiate), negotiate a compromise where necessary, or decide how each might have his/her own way. For example, each might be able to pursue a separate course that the other does not enjoy.

- If a couple is finding it difficult to come up with creative solutions to problems, a pre-retirement planning course might be able to offer some suggestions.

## How Your Income Affects Your Retirement Lifestyle

Income is obviously one of the major limiting factors with regard to the retirement lifestyle. For instance, studies have shown that when pre-retirees are asked what they would most like to do in retirement, they say travel. When retirees are asked what they *are doing,* the most common activity is watching television. One of the main reasons for this discrepancy is income.

However, when retirees are asked if their income is adequate to meet their needs, the majority say yes. This may be because people in retirement actually have reduced needs (no mortgage, no children to educate, no need for an extensive wardrobe). It may also be that people have reduced wants. The current retirees went through a period of economic depression in the 1930s that left many with the belief that all they need is adequate food, shelter and clothing.

Most people will retire with less — or considerably less — income than they had when they were employed. However, the real issue is not the lower income, but whether it is sufficient to maintain a standard of retirement living equivalent to the one enjoyed while you were working. Studies have shown that people earning between $25,000 and $50,000 a year before retirement will generally require between 50 per cent and 60 per cent of that amount to maintain their standard of living in retirement (the lower the earnings, the greater the percentage that will be required). This is due, in part, to the fact that many work-related expenses will be eliminated or greatly reduced with retirement, and, in part, because senior citizens are entitled to a variety of money-saving opportunities (such as free drugs and reduced fares on public transportation, depending on where they live). If the retirement income is not sufficient to maintain the pre-retirement lifestyle, some changes will obviously have to be made. The retiree can either seek additional sources of income (such as a part-time job), or try to reduce expenses, or decide to settle for a reduced lifestyle. The issue can be a complicated one. For instance, since housing is usually the largest fixed cost of the retiree, a move to less expensive accommodation might be one method of reducing expenses in order to maintain the current lifestyle. However, housing can greatly influence one's lifestyle. If people have lived for a long time in their current home, they may have a strong emotional attachment to that home, even if it is too expensive and too large. There may also be a network of friends in the neighbourhood. For some, a reduced standard of living may be more acceptable than maintaining the previous standard in a new location.

There are clearly no simple solutions for this kind of situation. The answers will vary from individual to individual. What is important is that a person faced with these kinds of choices carefully examine the different possibilities — *and their consequences* — before making decisions that could profoundly affect the retirement lifestyle.

## How Your Health Affects Your Retirement Lifestyle

In many ways, health has an even more immediate impact on lifestyle than income. Research has shown that more important than the number of health problems is the perception of how debilitating those problems are. For instance, one person with arthritis may shift from bicycling to swimming in order to reduce stress on knee joints, while another may decide that people with arthritis cannot do exercise and retire to an easy chair in front of the television.

The following exercise can be useful in looking at the impact of health problems upon activities, and ways to deal with the limitations:

• List any health problems that you have, i.e., arthritis, diabetes, hypertension.

• List any activities that you have reduced or given up because of any of these problems.

• Are there activities you are prevented from doing because of any of these health problems?

• What was the satisfaction you gained from the activities that have been reduced or given up?

• What other activities might you substitute that would replace that satisfaction?

This exercise requires some creativity. For instance, one woman had given up gardening because she could no longer maintain her large home and yard, but she began to grow beautiful orchids in a small solarium in her new condominium. Another woman who received great satisfaction from knitting sweaters for her grandchildren had to stop knitting because of arthritic hands; instead, she was able to give each grandchild one hour a week of her undivided attention.

## How to Handle Early Retirement

Early retirement is becoming much more common. While we still tend to consider any retirement before age 65 as "early", the average age of retirement is now about 63.

The characteristics of the satisfied early retiree might include the following:

• Answered yes to most of the questions on the Retirement Readiness Checklist.

• Chose to retire.

• Regards his/her income as adequate.

• Had specific plans for retirement activities (make wooden toys to sell through the Children's Boutique), as opposed to vague plans (do some woodworking).

• Has maintained contact with co-workers or has a group of friends who share retirement interests.

• Has no intention of returning to full-time employment.

Even if you are a good candidate for early retirement, there are some negative aspects to be considered.

- Depending upon your age at retirement, you could live 30 or more years, making your retirement longer than your working life. Some people are not prepared for such a lengthy retirement period.

- Depending upon your age, other people may think you are too young, lazy or merely unemployed.

- There may be few people of your age who are also retired. This may limit friendships.

- Your spouse may still be working, and intending to work for many more years. This could be a source of marital tension.

The person who, for whatever reason, was forced into retirement earlier than anticipated is in a different situation. Here, planning for retirement may well begin after the fact. If feasible, this person may want to explore other employment possibilities before deciding if he/she is in fact retired, or just currently unemployed. If the person is retired, developing specific, realistic plans for retirement activities can help to raise what could be a sagging morale.

# CHAPTER 3

# Roosting and the Empty Nest: Living Arrangements in Retirement

*If you survive long enough, you're revered — rather like an old building.*

Katharine Hepburn

When Canadians who are nearing retirement are asked what they believe their most important needs will be, they most often mention sufficient income, reasonably good health, and family and community supports. Rarely do these people mention housing or living arrangements. The same attitude prevails when people think of planning for retirement: Most are concerned about financial planning, and preparing for the use of more leisure time. Few people, it seems, regard their future living arrangements as an area that requires much thought.

Housing, however, can have a great influence on many aspects of your retirement life, as well as being closely related to the factors (income, health, community support, etc.) that *are* regarded as important. For instance, if your income is not sufficient it can be very difficult to maintain existing housing in good condition. If your housing is not conveniently located near community services, you could encounter problems in obtaining necessary health care or in taking advantage of social and recreational opportunities. Inadequate housing may even negatively affect your health, either by stimulating new problems or aggravating existing health conditions. For example, a person afflicted with asthma or other respiratory problems would find these conditions aggravated by housing that is badly ventilated, and a person with a heart condition such as angina might have difficulty living in accommodation where there are a lot of stairs to climb.

Thus, the issue of housing is — or should be — central to the process of retirement planning. The fact that it is largely overlooked may stem from the attitude that since each person or household now has a place to live — whether owned or rented — such accommodation will continue to be available and affordable in the future. In view of the changing economic conditions, this attitude may be entirely wrong. In fact, for most of us, the need to plan for living arrangements in retirement was never more important.

When planning for future housing and living arrangements, an individual or couple should take a number of different matters into consideration:

• The size of the household
• The cost of the housing accommodation
• Location (neighbourhood; proximity to friends, relatives, activities)
• Transportation facilities
• Community services, such as health and social agencies
• The likely status of your health and that of your spouse (based on the present state of health)

Decisions about living arrangements must be based on realistic thinking and not on vague prospects or pleasant dreams about the way you would live if only....

# THE COST OF ACCOMMODATION IN RETIREMENT

Planning about retirement accommodation must begin with a realistic appraisal of what the person or couple will be able to afford. This means that one must try to figure out what housing will likely cost in retirement and relate that to the probable income that will be available (see the chapter on "Taking it with You: Financial Planning for Retirement"). For many people, the housing options that are available in retirement will largely depend upon the nature and status of the pre-retirement living arrangements.

## Costs for Retired Home Owners

If you own your home, the first consideration is the costs that are likely to be involved on a monthly or yearly basis in retirement.

• Will there be a mortgage which still requires monthly payments for some years to come, or will that mortgage have been paid off in full?

• How much are the current taxes, and what will they be if they increase by 6 per cent each year? (This is the current trend in North American communities and is likely to continue in the future; in fact, 6 per cent might be a low estimate, but even that would result in a doubling of taxes in seven years.)

• What are the current costs for heating, electricity, water, and telephone, and what will these be if they too increase by 6 per cent each year, compounded into the future? (Again, considering the heavy increases in recent years in the costs of electricity, gas, and heating oil, this estimate might be low.)

• What repairs and replacement costs are likely to be needed over time? These costs are more difficult to estimate as they relate to the age and condition of the house and the probability of problems developing with such things as the furnace, the plumbing, the electrical system, and the roof. A fair approximation would be to add 10 per cent per year of all other costs.

## Costs for Retirees Who Rent

The basic costs for rented accommodation in the future might be slightly easier to calculate and will include the monthly (or weekly) rent, plus heating costs and utilities (gas, electricity, water) if these are not already included in the rent. If the rent does include everything, the basic expenses are then likely to be the monthly rent plus the cost of a telephone.

It is difficult to estimate what will happen with rents in the future. For the present, in many parts of Canada, rental accommodation is under some form of rent control or rent review. While this has helped significantly to stabilize rents, there is still at least a 6 per cent increase in the rent each year. Also, as it is far from certain that the controls will continue indefinitely, it might be safer to assume that average rentals will increase by at least 10 per cent per year over the next ten or twenty years.

## Accommodation Costs and Your Retirement Income

Once your future housing costs have been estimated, they can be compared to your anticipated retirement income. There used to be an old rule that a person should not pay more than a week's wages for a month's rent. When home ownership became more common, this rule was translated to become: No one should pay more than about 20 per cent of monthly income for shelter cost. By the mid-1960s, many people were accepting the view that perhaps 25 per cent of income, or even 30 per cent, should be devoted to shelter. And there are even people — usually younger couples — who spend as much as 35 per cent of their gross monthly income in meeting the costs of home ownership.

At the same time, unfortunately, there are also many older people who are spending as much as 40 to 50 per cent of their monthly income to meet the costs of home ownership. When such large proportions of income are devoted to meeting basic shelter costs, it is clear that all other areas of a normal budget will be affected negatively and that the standard of living will be significantly reduced. Not only is it difficult, if not impossible, to participate in leisure activities that involve cost, it is also not uncommon for people in these circumstances to go without adequate nutrition, proper clothing, or even such essential items as good dental care. This sort of denial can seriously affect one's health, either by aggravating existing medical problems, or by creating new ones.

The same situation can affect retirees who rent. If the rental is going to mean more than 25 per cent or 30 per cent of the anticipated monthly income, then it may not be affordable.

However, because there is a drastic shortage of rental accommodation in many parts of Canada, you might have to plan to spend at least 30 per cent of your monthly income on shelter costs, or even 35 per cent if the rental includes heat, electricity, and water. If the rent does not include these items, it should probably not exceed 25 per cent of your income, to allow leeway for these other necessary living expenses.

People whose anticipated housing costs will be more than 30 per cent of their income have some difficult issues to face, for which there will not always be satisfactory solutions. While a move to less expensive housing may be indicated, in many parts of Canada there is, as already mentioned, a great shortage of reasonably priced accommodation, and it may not be possible to locate decent housing that is truly affordable. For this reason, the further in advance that planning for the retirement living arrangements is begun, the better off one is likely to be. The last decade before retirement, or even much earlier, if possible, is by no means too soon to begin planning.

For those people who do find themselves caught in difficult circumstances, there are several possibilities that might be explored:

- In nearly every province there are "seniors only" public housing developments and/or provincially subsidized non-profit housing. In these programs, rents are frequently geared to income, and are thus more affordable. The difficulty is that demand for this accommodation far exceeds supply, and there are often very long waiting lists to get in.

- For homeowners, there are programs in most provinces that provide grants or loans to seniors to make repairs or home improvements. Eligibility is generally related to income, but for retired homeowners who meet the requirements, these programs offer a way either to maintain their homes, or to cope with emergencies that might arise.

- For renters, there are programs in some provinces that offer rental assistance or rent supplements for seniors. Eligibility is again linked to income. For those who qualify, the programs make up the difference by which the rent exceeds a certain percentage (usually 30 per cent) of monthly income. Thus, these programs help to keep housing affordable for those with very limited income.

## Location and Transportation Needs in Retirement

After cost, the location of your accommodation is one of the most important considerations in retirement. Real estate agents like to say that the three most important factors in selling a house are "location, location, and location." This repetition emphasizes the importance — for both buyers and sellers — of the house being well-located with respect to schools, churches, hospitals, shopping facilities, transportation, and other services such as physicians' and dentists'. For retirees, the location of their housing is at least as significant — and possibly more significant — as it is for young families buying their first house.

As a person grows older, the question of whether he or she is able to carry out what are known as "the activities of daily living" becomes an increasingly important concern. If the home is reasonably close to the facilities mentioned above, it is easier for an older person to carry on such activities as shopping, banking, attending church, appointments with a physician or dentist, and so on. Even if one is not well enough at some point to do these activities, it can still be fairly easy to secure deliveries or to receive help from family or friends, if the tasks to be carried out are reasonably close at hand.

Closely related to the matter of location is the availability of transportation facilities, the importance of which cannot be overstated. While many older people own automobiles, the cost of driving and maintaining a car has risen steeply since the early 1970s, and these costs can strain a limited retirement budget. On the other hand, many communities offer senior citizens reduced fares on public transportation. Therefore, when evaluating your anticipated retirement living arrangements — regardless of whether the intention is to stay or move — the nearness of a bus or subway route can be a major consideration. For those who are handicapped or have illnesses affecting their mobility, the availability in a community of special transportation facilities for the elderly should also be investigated.

Without the availability of public transportation, or the capacity to drive an automobile in inclement weather — particularly the Canadian winter — older people can be forced to remain at home. If you are single, you may become more or less cut off from social contacts, and the lack of transportation facilities can contribute substantially to a weakened capacity to take care of yourself.

If your present accommodation was purchased or rented at a time when you were young and physically fit, you might not have paid much attention to the convenience of the location or the question of transportation. However, people planning for retirement should look carefully at these issues. Even if the financial arrangements are attractive — either for the current dwelling or the anticipated one — an inconvenient location can more than offset other advantages.

## TO STAY OR MOVE IN RETIREMENT

Nearly every person nearing retirement will at some point consider — or be asked by friends, family, and associates — where he or she will live after retirement. While there may be many individual responses to this question, the possibilities are basically to stay, buy, or rent. If the present home is owned, it can be retained, or the retiree(s) can sell it and either buy a new house or move into rental accommodation. If the present accommodation is rented, the retiree(s) can stay, rent somewhere else, or purchase a house or condominium.

Whether to stay or move is one of the most important choices to be made in retirement, for the decision will influence many other aspects of your life. It is not at all uncommon for retired people who have moved, to greatly regret the decision. Even more, it has been found that, for older people, significant changes in living arrangements may be so difficult or prove to be so emotionally upsetting that their health — or even their life span — may be negatively affected.

For these reasons, experts recommend that where there is a choice, the choice should always be to stay rather than to move. Obviously, this does not mean that every retirement move is a failure, or that there are not good reasons for a move. What it means is that, since it's generally better *not to move*, it's extremely important to examine both the reasons to move, and the possible consequences of that move.

Financial considerations are, of course, one of the central issues to be taken into account, but there are also many other factors that need to be examined. The following are some of the questions that anyone contemplating a move should think about:

## TO MOVE OR STAY — A CHECKLIST

• Are you ready to move, or are you still strongly attached to your present home?

• Do you really want to move and are you looking forward to the change? Or is it that you think you should make a change, because retirement is a time that involves fundamental changes?

• Are you well enough — in both physical and emotional terms — to undertake the tasks of packing up your belongings, moving to a new location, and unpacking once again?

• Is your current accommodation really too large for your purposes? This is the main reason for moving, especially if the house or apartment was used to raise a family, and the children are now grown and have moved out.

• Are you certain that the new accommodation will have enough room? If you're married, is there an extra room in case you or your spouse becomes ill and has to sleep alone? Is there space in which children or grandchildren can stay for a visit?

• Have you carefully calculated *all* the costs of the contemplated living arrangements, and can you afford it?

• Have you carefully calculated *all* the costs of the move itself? These can include legal fees and land transfer tax if you're buying a house, moving costs (which can easily be considerable), and such things as the purchase of new appliances and furniture.

• How convenient is the new location? Is it close to your children, your church or synagogue, your doctor, your friends, and your recreational activities?

• What are the public transportation facilities in the new location? How difficult will it be to continue the activities that you consider necessary or important?

---

In order to avoid mistakes or unpleasant surprises, these are the kinds of questions that must be carefully considered *before* a move is made. It can sometimes be very helpful to have a lawyer or a close friend ask these questions — and to make sure that your answers are satisfactory.

Like all other decisions concerning your retirement, the decision to move or stay should be made early. Staying in your current accommodation may require extensive modifications to your surroundings. While you may find that you will take enormous pleasure in becoming an inveterate do-it-yourselfer in retirement, you should be aware now of what that might involve. What will you do with the kids' rooms? Will you be happy wrestling bundles of insulation into the attic, cording wood for the winter, painting, and adapting your old space to your new needs? Perhaps, but let us assume not.

The Canada Mortgage and Housing Corporation provides information on how to make your home safer and more liveable and on how to find contractors to do the work. It also offers financial assistance under the Residential Rehabilitation Assistance Program for eligible alteration (a brochure is available; see "Further Reading"). Your local community information centre will be able to assist you in investigating support services available in your area, such as Meals on Wheels, Chronic Home Care, Homemaker Services, and municipal snow removal. The ministries of consumer and corporate affairs can provide information on adapting your living environment to suit the disabled, including funding available for this purpose.

Although it may be better wherever possible to stay instead of move, there are obviously circumstances where a move is indicated. For instance, the present house or apartment may truly be too large, too difficult to look after, require too many repairs, or be too expensive to maintain. However, even in this situation it may be possible to stay by renting out some of the extra space, and thereby gain enough extra income to make the house affordable. This option will be discussed later in the chapter. Some provinces have programs that provide financial aid to those wishing to convert part of a single-family dwelling to rental accommodation.

The decision to move also depends upon the age of the people concerned, the family circumstances, and the nature of the relationships with friends, religious affiliations, and so on.

• The older one is, the more difficult the move will be. Thus if one is inclined to move, it is far better to do it in the early years of retirement than to wait a decade when one's physical and emotional resources might well be considerably reduced.

- If the children have moved away, out of the particular community into another city, the decision to move may be strengthened because the retirees will not find themselves any farther away from their children and grandchildren than they are at present.

- As neighbourhoods change, old friends and neighbours move away, and the membership of religious and social associations turns over. A major reason to stay — the support system of family and friends — may no longer apply, and a move may not result in significant losses in those areas.

## WHETHER TO BUY A HOUSE OR RENT IN RETIREMENT

If the decision to move has been made, the question then becomes whether to buy or rent the new accommodation. The issues involved here could differ somewhat, depending upon whether the present accommodation is owned or rented.

### Buying a Home in Retirement

For many people, their major asset may very well be the house that they own. If the mortgage has been paid off, the costs of accommodation will include only the local property taxes, heating, utilities, and upkeep (both normal wear and tear and any necessary major repairs). This could mean that one's housing costs will be very reasonable in retirement, a good reason not to move.

On the other hand, the house might be too large or too costly to maintain, or perhaps there are no longer any strong ties to the neighbourhood or even to the city. At the same time, considering what has happened to the price of real estate in recent years, the value of the house may well have increased substantially. It could be worth a large amount of money, and if the house is the principal residence, the capital gains that a sale would realize would not be taxable. (This is discussed more fully in the chapter "Taking It With You: Financial Planning for Retirement"). Under these circumstances it might make sense to sell and buy a smaller, more convenient house.

There is an assumption, made by many current owners, that security for the future is simply a matter of remortgaging the home or, as it is called in financial circles, "home equity conversion". A word of caution seems in order, however. It is often costly to "unlock" the equity in your house because the financial plans required are complex, as they are tied to fluctuations in mortgage and inflation rates and the additional income generated is often insignificant in net worth once these costs have been incurred. Therefore, if you have assumed that remortgaging is the answer for you, it would be a good idea to talk to an expert before going ahead.

After determining that factors such as the location and size of the new residence will meet your requirements, both current and for some time into the future, there are several other issues that should be closely examined:

---

## A BUYING CHECKLIST

• Will you be able to purchase the new home outright with the proceeds from the sale of your present home? Just as the value of your house has risen, so has that of other houses. The very cost of a new home may seem staggering compared to the cost of purchase in the 1940s or 1950s... or even 1960s.

• Will the proceeds of the sale cover all the costs of the new purchase? These could include legal fees, land transfer tax, moving costs, and other unforeseen expenses. If not, how much will you be out of pocket, and can you afford it?

• Will the proceeds of the sale cover any repairs or renovations you might want to make to the new residence? Will the proceeds cover any new purchases that might be required or desired, such as appliances and furniture?

• How do the monthly operating costs (taxes, heat, utilities, condominium maintenance charges, etc.) compare to those of your present house? What are they likely to be in the future, and how do they compare to your anticipated retirement income?

---

If the home to be purchased costs more than will be realized by selling the present house, it will be necessary to take out a mortgage. Some people in this position might be in for a rude shock. Even though interest rates are down from the 18 per cent or 19 per cent of the early 1980s, they still are about double what they were twenty or thirty years ago. The whole question of a mortgage should be explored very thoroughly by shopping around from bank to bank, from trust company to lending institution, to find out exactly what the rates will be on one-, two-, three-, and five-year mortgages. The monthly mortgage costs should then be added to the other operating costs and related to the anticipated retirement income. Some consideration should also be given to what one's position will be if interest rates again skyrocket at some point in the future. Inflation rates can vary considerably and, upon reflection, you might decide that taking out a mortgage could be too risky an undertaking.

Besides interest rates there are other costs involved in taking out a mortgage that must be kept in mind. Some banks or lending institutions insist that the borrower utilize lawyers of their choice — either on their staff or in private practice — and pay the fee. There are also appraisals to be carried out by a specialist chosen by the bank or lending institution, and the borrower is also responsible for those fees. The bank may charge some other fees as well that are involved with the preparation of documents. In all, the fees might amount to two thousand dollars or more. However, some lending institutions will permit the borrower to use his or her own lawyer, and will not charge more than a standard appraisal fee of about $250 or $300. Whether small or large, these are all costs that a prospective purchaser must take into account and relate to his or her available resources.

You may have already considered selling your primary residence and moving to the family cottage or farm as a retirement option. If so, you will undoubtedly have already considered factors such as location, transportation, isolation from others, and maintenance demands. Country life has significant appeal for a large number of people who see it as the idyllic reward for a life spent toiling in urban surroundings. However, you should be aware that, while the life of laird and lady may be peaceful and rewarding for a couple in the early years of retirement, it may become untenable in later years, most particularly for those who lose a spouse or are forced to adapt to any kind of disability.

## Renting Accommodation in Retirement

The most obvious alternative to buying a new house is to move into an apartment or other rental accommodation. Looking at the current value of his or her house, a homeowner might decide to sell, pocketing a large capital sum, and use the income from the interest on the capital to pay the rent. Once again, however, a long-time homeowner might well be in for some unpleasant surprises. Just as the value of the house has risen greatly, so too has the cost of renting an apartment. Compared to what the retiree might have known twenty or thirty years before, current rentals may seem absolutely staggering. Also, given the shortage of rental accommodation that exists in many areas, it could be a problem just finding an apartment, let alone an affordable one.

Besides the question of size, location, nearness to friends and services, and availability of public transportation that anyone considering a move should ask, there are other questions that a homeowner thinking about renting should consider:

---

## RENTAL CHECKLIST

• How much can you hope to realize from the sale of your house, after paying commissions and various other costs?

• Can you find an apartment in a well-maintained building in a good location that you can rent for the interest on the capital generated by the sale? For instance, if you earn 10 per cent by putting the money into Term Deposits or Guaranteed Interest Certificates (so as to maintain the greatest security), will there be enough income *after tax* to pay the rent entirely?

• If not included in the rent, how much will water, gas, electricity and heat cost each month? Will the amount you earn in interest *after tax* cover these costs as well?

• What is the record of rent increases (the percentage increase) over the last three or four years? What will that percentage mean projected into the future?

• Under the terms of the lease, will there be other costs involved in occupying the apartment? For instance, does the landlord expect you to buy furniture, carpeting or fixtures as a condition of granting a lease?

• What is the new neighbourhood like? It may be conveniently located, but what is the situation with regard to parking, traffic, and the matter of noise? People moving from a quiet residential neighbourhood to a centrally located apartment may discover unanticipated problems in these respects.

---

One further point should be made with regard to paying rent. While it is clearly not necessary that it be paid only out of interest earnings, most people tend to think in these terms. First of all, there is a sense of security in knowing that there is a large capital sum on deposit in some financial institution. That sense of security might be diminished if it is necessary to dip into capital every month. If you are coming from a situation where the mortgage had been paid off and housing costs involved only taxes, utilities, and necessary repairs, it may seem unnatural to be using savings to pay rent. Furthermore, many people are unhappy with the idea that they are reducing the estate that they will one day leave for their children, grandchildren, or other relatives.

The above are the kinds of issues that require the careful attention of anyone considering selling his or her house and moving into an apartment. Even if all the answers to these questions are satisfactory, it is likely that it will be at least as difficult — if not more difficult — to find a suitable rental location as it would be to find a suitable house to purchase with the proceeds of the sale of the present house.

## Costs for Tenants in Retirement

While the purchase of a new house in retirement is a serious issue that requires a good deal of thought and planning for anyone contemplating it, people who are currently renting their accommodation must exercise even more caution. Not only must they ask all the questionss given above, but they must also pay particular attention to the financial ramifications of a purchase. It is sometimes believed that people who have been tenants for many years have thereby saved a great deal of money (compared to homeowners who must meet mortgages, taxes, repairs, etc.), and, thus, are easily able to buy a home. Unfortunately, this can be very far from the truth, because older tenants lack the major asset — the house — that can be sold, the proceeds of which will go towards the purchase of a new house. For these people, therefore, buying a house may involve an intolerable financial burden.

## Buying a Condominium

Tenants frequently consider the purchase of a condominium an increasingly popular form of dwelling because of the advantages it offers. Retirees feel a condominium offers the assets of a house without the need to do heavy maintenance or keep up repairs. They appreciate the security arrangements, especially if they travel a great deal, and the social life and exercise facilities are also appealing factors in condominium life.

A condominium is simply an apartment or house that is jointly owned with a number of other people, each of whom is the owner of a unit within the complex. While individual owners own their own accommodation, they *jointly* own all of the common space, including exterior space. In most provinces, the condominium purchasers must form an association, elect officers, and make democratic decisions about such things as the hiring of superintendents, janitors, parking attendants, and the people responsible for the upkeep and landscaping of the exterior. The joint costs, which a prospective owner may not have anticipated, can amount to a substantial addition on top of the monthly mortgage costs, and there is no certainty that the expenditures will not increase in the future. Therefore, a tenant or couple considering the purchase of a condominium apartment should probably be in the upper middle income group in retirement, with a total annual income of $35,000 to $50,000.

The tenant who plans to continue renting in retirement must look at all the issues previously mentioned. If the intention is to remain in the current apartment, the tenant must determine his or her capacity to pay the rent with the retirement income, re-evaluate the location of the apartment with respect to planned retirement activities, and consider the ease or difficulty with which family and friends can visit or be visited. If the intention is to move to another apartment, the tenant will have all of these concerns, as well as the more general problems brought about by the shortage of affordable rental accommodations in many regions.

## THE IMPORTANCE OF PERSONALITY AND PREFERENCES IN CHOOSING LIVING ARRANGEMENTS

Ultimately, many of the decisions that have to be made regarding retirement living arrangements will be influenced by the personality and preferences of those doing the deciding. While the balance sheet may indicate that some changes are necessary, the individual feelings and attitudes that are part of one's personality also have to be taken into consideration when making decisions about such important matters as whether to move or stay, whether to buy or rent.

A simple way of thinking about *personality* is that it is your "distinctive personal character". *Preference* is the "liking of one thing more than another". A person must really understand himself or herself when making decisions concerning future living arrangements. For instance, a person might prefer to live in a neighbourhood in which the houses are close together, but at the same time value his or her privacy, and not like to engage in gossip and over-the-fence conversation with the neighbours. This is a simple example of how a preference must be modified by an understanding of one's personal character.

Nearly everyone knows people who misjudge their own characters — people, for instance, who think they are easy-going and able to adjust smoothly to changing circumstances, but who, in reality, are not flexible and cannot easily adjust. For a person like this, a move from one form of accommodation to another could cause difficulties, generate stress, and even be injurious. Because this issue is important, it may be useful for individuals or couples to seek the help of others in assessing their personal characteristics before firmly deciding to change their living arrangements. The people most able to help in making this kind of assessment could include the minister, priest or rabbi, social workers in a family agency, the supervisors or program directors in a community centre for seniors, and perhaps trusted friends or neighbours. An outsider may well be in a better position to ask the questions that will reflect disparities between preferences and personalities, between wishful thinking and the reality of personal needs and characteristics.

The significant questions concern the matter of flexibility, and very basic habits or patterns of living can reveal a great deal. Does the person set the table and sit down when it is time to eat? Does the person clear off the dishes following the meal and either wash them right away or put them in the dishwasher? Does the person clean the house regularly, and insist on tidiness — such as always hanging up clothes and maintaining a clean bathroom — from his or her spouse? If one is somewhat more flexible in these matters, it might mean that the presence of a tenant in the house would not necessarily be terribly disruptive. Conversely, if a person were rigidly neat and tidy, insisting that everything be in its place, the presence of another person — or living in some kind of group or co-operative housing arrangement — might be intolerable.

## LIVING WITH OTHER PEOPLE IN RETIREMENT

During the pre-retirement years, people do not usually plan to move on the day of retirement, or the next day, or even during the next year. Upon retirement, most people are reasonably healthy, and have a sufficient income to maintain their current living habits for some time, if not indefinitely. Changes made at this time will be largely voluntary — the result of choices by the individual or the household — and if the matter has been well thought out beforehand, there is no reason why the changes shouldn't be successful.

It is during the second decade of retirement (age 75 to 84) that the necessity of making some changes in one's living arrangements becomes more common (although this is by no means always the case). The need for change could be due to failing health, the loss of friends or acquaintances, or the loss of one's spouse. Whereas one might have been living independently before, moves at this time frequently involve situations where one will be living with other people or households.

The following are some of the most common alternatives of this sort. While these kinds of moves may be somewhat less voluntary than those undertaken earlier, there is still frequently room for choice. Many of the issues of the planning process still apply and, as the new arrangements often involve close contact with other people, particular attention should be given to one's own preferences and personality.

### Shared Living

Although the concept of house sharing is not unfamiliar to the present generation of elderly people in Canada — during their youth it was fairly common for families to take in lodgers — today it is a lifestyle more commonly associated with the young.

It can, however, in certain circumstances, be an attractive option for older people. For example, many retired homeowners tend to own their homes outright but still bear the burden of heavy maintenance costs. For some, the size of the house, built for family living, now provides more space than they can comfortably handle. Many of these retired homeowners are likely to be widowed females whose inability to afford the costs of maintenance is compounded by loneliness and failing health. Although living alone becomes increasingly difficult for these homeowners, they are often unwilling to give up the feeling of independence that comes from owning their own property. They also have strong emotional attachments to the community and house which offer continuity with the past.

House sharing, which in its basic form involves two unrelated individuals sharing a dwelling owned by one of them, could be the solution for certain of the elderly. It can range from a simple boarding house arrangement in which a tenant occupies bedroom space only, to a communal arrangement in which financial, social and household chores are shared more or less equally among the participants.

If there are owners who are having trouble making ends meet, there are also potential sharers who are also finding retirement difficult because of the high cost of rented accommodation. Take, for example, the case of a widow who, although finding her house costly to maintain, did not wish to leave it. Meanwhile a retired secretary was finding it difficult to make the payments for rent in her apartment. When the secretary became the widow's tenant, their loneliness was resolved along with their financial problems.

Of course, there is no situation that is perfect and a close look should be taken at the disadvantages as well as the advantages which are presented in the following table:

## ADVANTAGES AND DISADVANTAGES OF SHARED HOUSING

| Advantages | Disadvantages |
| --- | --- |
| • Financial benefits | • Loss of privacy |
| • Companionship | • Sharer may have to move from own community |
| • Social integration | • Physical design of property |
| • Task sharing | • Incompatibility |
| • Remain in own community | • Policy deterrants, e.g., planning regulations |
| • Reduces fear | |
| • Intergenerational house sharing brings young and old closer together | |
| • Inexpensive to implement | |

Adapted from: S.R. McConnell and C.E. Usher, *Intergenerational House-Sharing: A Research Report and Resource Manual.* Los Angeles: University of Southern California, Andrus Gerontology Center (1980), p. 5.

The financial benefits as well as companionship are probably the two most important advantages of house sharing. However, the kind of relationship that develops between house sharers will depend totally on their compatibility. Sometimes house sharing matches work out better when the participants are from two different generations. For example, a widow in failing health might want to share her house with a university student who does the heavier chores as part of the arrangement for her accommodation.

Before you consider house sharing it would be wise to make an honest assessment of your temperament. Can you handle the disruption and lack of privacy another person might cause in your home? What do you need in exchange for sharing your house? What age and type of person would be able to fulfill those needs for you? Is your house set up physically so that space can be divided in a way that pleases both you and your tenant?

If, after the proper soul searching, you do decide to share your house, be sure that the needs of both parties are made clear from the outset. Take your time about finding the right tenant. After all, it could be the beginning of a lifetime friendship.

## Retirement Homes

In many Canadian cities there are residential buildings that are utilized as "retirement homes". These are operated by private business for profit, and usually offer living accommodation, meals, some general care, and leisure activities for a daily fee, which may be as much as $50 or $75. The standard of care should be relatively high, and if residents become ill, they will either receive care from professionals on call or be transferred to a hospital.

Some of these retirement homes are centrally located, but more often they are found on the outskirts of the city or in suburban areas, some distance from the traditional downtown core. There are also retirement homes that are part of a health care complex in which a nursing home is the major facility. In these cases, people are sometimes transferred from the retirement home to the nursing home for more intensive care, either for short periods or longer terms.

## Group Homes

A group home is simply a variation of a retirement home, but sponsored by a social agency or a community group, and the residents usually have some affiliation with the sponsoring organization. The nature of the services and activities within the home are very much like those in private retirement homes, but the rates are likely to be much lower than in homes operated for a profit.

## Retirement Communities

In some parts of Canada developers have built housing subdivisions they designate as "retirement communities". These towns or villages are usually adjacent to a small town, and near a traditional recreational centre such as Ontario's Georgian Bay. The homes within the community are for sale (very little rental accommodation, if any, is available), and the facilities usually include a golf course, tennis courts and often a social or recreation centre.

## Moving to the Sun Belt

The most popular fantasy about retirement living, particularly for Canadians, is moving to the Sun Belt. The retirement communities that Canadians most often read about are in Florida, California, Arizona and other parts of the southern and south-western United States.

A favourable climate is, of course, the chief appeal and retired people who buy into these communities usually plan to spend most of the year in that location. However, as with any major move in your life, investigation and planning are essential before you follow the sun into a new way of life.

## The Lure of the Sun

When the temperature is 66°F with a relative humidity of about 55 per cent, your body chemistry functions at maximum efficiency and without strain. You may not have known that particular fact but you do know that you feel better, both physically and mentally, in a climate where gentle breezes blow and the sun beams down. Many people retire to the Sun Belt specifically because they want to feel healthier.

Stress diseases such as ulcers, certain heart problems, and hardening of the arteries are less frequent in warmer zones. Older people suffering from arthritis, rheumatism, emphysema, and respiratory problems will find the states of Arizona and New Mexico to be true havens.

If health reasons are among the major priorities for a move south, it would be wise to consult your doctor first, as he or she knows your medical history and can help you to evaluate the move. Make sure that your new home in the sun has doctors and hospitals available. In some rural areas in the United States there is a desperate shortage of doctors and some towns are now pleading for doctors to settle in them.

Even if you are in good health, you should thoroughly investigate the possible costs of illness when you are living outside of Canada. Take as an example the unhappy story of Bill and Sue Jones. When they retired a few years ago, they moved to South Carolina. They loved it—the beautiful scenery, inexpensive housing, and a nearby golf course were all very appealing. They were also well set financially. They had sold their Canadian house for $100,000 and paid only $40,000 for their South Carolina home. Then, a few years later, the Canadian dollar plunged in value and, because they were receiving Canadian pensions, the difference between the Canadian and U.S. dollar began to hurt them. They could still manage, though, by cutting back on a few pleasures. However, some time later, Bill suffered a heart attack and it was discovered he needed a triple bypass operation. Both Bill and Sue had health insurance but, as they discovered, their insurance scheme paid only $10,500 toward the operation. The hospital bill totalled $40,000. They are now in serious financial trouble and without the necessary funds to move back to Canada. The moral of the story: Take every possible eventuality into consideration, no matter how depressing it may be to contemplate, before you plan a move south.

## The Tax Implications for Relocation

For Canadians who retire to the U.S. and become U.S. residents, there are significant tax implications that should be examined closely. Recent changes in the U.S. tax law and the Canada-U.S. Tax Treaty may also affect Canadians who do not become residents of the U.S. but who own winter homes there.

Generally, spending more than six months a year in the U.S. makes you liable for tax in the U.S. as a resident, and that means the U.S. will tax your worldwide income from all sources. Moreover, the definition of a resident in the U.S. has recently been expanded to include anyone with an immigrant visa and anyone who spends more than 31 days in the country if substantial amounts of time have been spent there in prior years. However, at the moment, the new Canada-U.S. Tax Treaty still protects Canadians who spend less than 183 days in the U.S. and who have closer ties to, and pay tax to, Canada.

If you become a non-resident of Canada, under the new Tax Treaty, the withholding tax is 15% on most pensions and 25% on annuities from Canadian RRSPs. Added to this are Canadian withholding taxes on Canadian source interest dividends and estate income.

You should also be aware that unless your U.S. property is held in a Canadian company, it will be subject to U.S. probate and estate taxation in the event of death. As the basic exemption is only $60,000, U.S. estate taxes can be considerable. For example, on an estate of $1 million, the U.S. estate tax is about $350,000 while in Canada there is no estate tax as such.

It should also be remembered that the Canadian tax system, in contrast to the U.S., favours older people. Canadian tax preferences such as the dividend tax credit, the $1,000 Canadian investment income and pension deductions or larger personal exemptions for older people make the Canadian tax system more attractive than U.S. taxation.

As can be seen from the above, careful study and planning must be taken when retired Canadians are deciding whether or not to take up residence in the Sun Belt.

For those Canadians who decide to live in the U.S. as non-residents, but who still want to buy property and rent it for part of the year, there are important changes in the new treaty which should also be considered. After 1985, the U.S. rate of withholding tax on rent paid to Canadians rises from 15% to 30%. This tax can be avoided if Canadians report the regular net income tax of the rental property to the U.S. tax authorities. The normal operating costs and interest depreciation claimed for this purpose ordinarily result in no U.S. tax. If Canadians neglect to do this, they can remain exposed to an assessment of U.S. withholding tax on their total rental income.

## Housing in the Sun Belt

Because they do not need full basements for central heating systems, insulation or enclosed garages, houses in the Sun Belt tend to be much cheaper than in Canada. If you have decided that you want to live in the south, here are a few tips to follow before committing yourself to the financial outlay a house will entail:

— Pinpoint the area most suitable for your health, social, recreational and financial needs.

— Write to the specific state units on aging, located in the state capital, and ask about the locality and availability of housing, cost of living, taxes, climate, facilities and possible tax exemptions for seniors.

— Write to the local chamber of commerce. If you hear back and they are enthusiastic, you will know the welcome mat is out.

— Subscribe to the area's newspapers. You will learn a great deal about the community that way.

— Vacation in the area and get to know the people. When you are there, try to size up the community. Find out if the hospital is big enough—there should be five beds per 1,000 people. If you have health problems, are there specialists available? Is there much pollution or noise? Is there adequate shopping, good police protection and public transportation? Are there good banking, postal, legal and civic services?

— Rent instead of buying a house if you move south, and rent your house in Canada. In this way, if things are not working out for you, you can always move back.

## Social and Leisure Activities

If you are not the type of person who likes to get involved with people or group activities, you will be decidedly out of place in a Florida retirement community. Most people who retire to Sun Belt communities like the fact that personal interaction is based on social rather than economic status, but if being called a "good ol' boy" makes you shudder, do some hard thinking about a move to a southern retirement community. Similarly, if you are not the outdoors type or a nature enthusiast, moving to the Sun Belt would probably be a serious mistake.

For those who like a relaxed, informal, friendly and outdoor life, there are still some things you should check out before you move into a community. Are there libraries, museums, theatres, and art galleries? After all, you cannot play golf all the time. Are there educational opportunities for seniors or craft and hobby courses? Will you find the outdoor recreations appealing?

As you can see, there is a large amount of investigating to do before you decide whether your fantasy of a life in the sun will work for you. The nearest United States consulate can provide you with information about the legal aspects of relocation. There are also books available that deal with Sun Belt retirement although, unfortunately, they are primarily by Americans, for Americans (see "Further Reading"). Now is the time to find out if life in the sun will be right for you; after all, not all of us were meant to ripen in the sun like a raisin.

## Senior Citizens Housing Accommodation

In most Canadian cities and towns, there is likely to be some apartment accommodation built under federal-provincial-municipal agreements within the scope of the National Housing Act solely for the use of elderly individuals or couples. These apartments are for rental only, and to qualify, the prospective tenant(s) must have a low or moderate income and be living presently in accommodation that is more or less unsuitable.

The major benefit of this sort of accommodation is that the monthly rent is scaled to the income of the tenant, and generally does not exceed 25 per cent of gross income. The rents are thus much lower than in the private market and are quite reasonable from the point of view of the tenants. The apartments may be small — bachelors or one-bedrooms — but unlike retirement homes, each apartment has its own kitchen and bathroom. There are usually some leisure-time activities within the complex, but health care is the responsibility of the tenant.

Information about this form of accommodation can be obtained from the Senior Citizens Advisory Council in each province, from local community information centres, and from the local offices of Canada Mortgage and Housing. Upon application, the administration of the local or provincial housing authority will send an interviewer to the applicant's current residence to rate his or her priority based on income, health problems, and the inadequacy of the current dwelling. Unfortunately, demand for such accommodation far exceeds supply, and there may be a long waiting list and a delay of as many as two or three years to gain admission.

## Co-operative Apartments

Because condominiums and co-operatives are relatively recent types of accommodation, there is often confusion about the differences between them. In a condominium, you *own* your own unit as well as a portion of that property that you have in common with other owners (hallways, parking areas, recreation facilities and others areas). You buy the unit, pay the down payment and arrange the mortgage as you would in any ownership agreement. In addition to the monthly mortgage, there is a stipulated sum for the maintenance of the exterior of the building and of the common elements. This sum is proportional to the size of the unit owned.

In a co-op, you *do not* own your unit, but a share (or shares) in the corporation which, in turn, owns the entire project. The monthly fee will be proportional to the size of the unit and necessary maintenance fees are added.

In both types of accommodation, the majority rules: you pay for alterations and additions agreed to by the membership and you agree to abide by all regulations which may change as the needs of the residents change.

In many Canadian cities and towns, organizations have been formed to build co-operative housing under specific terms of the National Housing Act. These groups are usually founded by a union, a church, an ethnic association, or a lodge such as the Rotary Club. With the help of an architect and other advisers, these groups develop a plan to create a residential building. The government of Canada will provide grants to meet the fees of the architect and other planners, and to help the association meet the planning requirements of the city or town.

Each member of the co-operative who decides to move into the completed housing must put down a deposit of perhaps $1000 (refundable with interest if the member eventually moves out). While participants in a co-operative housing development are part-owners of the co-operative, they cannot achieve capital gains by selling their units, which must be turned back to the association if they move out. On the other hand, costs in a co-operative development tend to be lower than in the private sector due to government assistance, often in the form of a guaranteed mortgage at a considerably reduced rate. Furthermore, costs in a co-operative development tend to remain constant — or even decrease — over time, as the mortgage is gradually retired.

Co-operative projects can require a great deal of time and work on the part of the participants, both in the planning and development stages, and in the running of the completed project. Members must meet regularly to make decisions about the administration of the co-operative, such as the hiring of staff, maintenance needs such as cleaning and making repairs, and all the other day-to-day business. Although the process can be very rewarding, it can also be frustrating and time-consuming; thus, anyone thinking of participating in a co-operative should carefully consider whether he or she has the right personality and sufficient interest for his or her involvement to be successful.

The Co-operative Housing Federation has branches in the major cities and can provide information and assistance to groups and individuals interested in exploring this housing alternative. Labour Councils in many cities are also involved in the co-operative movement and are able to offer advice and assistance.

## Moving In with a Relative

Mary's mother has spent the summers with Mary's family since she was widowed three years earlier. Mother has strong opinions about the running of a household, formed over many years, and is frequently tyrannical in trying to enforce them. Mary's husband has equally strong feelings about his overt generosity in providing for Mother and about his position of authority in his family. Mary is juggling feelings of guilt, responsibility, and hostility from all quarters, and the kids are miserable. While this is not exactly a portrait of an ideal extended family, it could be a preview of what is in store for those of us who assume the kids will take us in when the time comes.

The decision to make this sort of move — which is difficult to reverse if the arrangement does not work out satisfactorily — must be taken with great care. An older person who believes that it is a very simple matter to move into the household of a married son or daughter may be very naive, even foolish. The success or failure of the move depends entirely on the personal characteristics of all the parties involved, and these must be examined very carefully. In cases where such a move is contemplated, it would be a very good idea for the older person to discuss the matter with outsiders — friends, a religious leader, a social worker in a senior centre — to get advice about the strengths and weaknesses of the proposed arrangement. The questions that should be asked are whether all the parties involved really want the move, and whether reduced privacy and/or independence will be a factor. A move that seems to make sense for reasons of companionship or finances might easily fail for reasons of personality and preference.

# The Risks and Benefits of Living with Others

In a way, any change in living arrangements is a move into uncharted waters. However, an awareness beforehand of the risks and potential problems can help to avoid unpleasant surprises after it is too late. This is true for any move, but especially for the housing alternatives discussed above, as these will represent a very fundamental change in living arrangements for most people. If at all possible, it would be advisable to spend some time visiting the contemplated residence, and talking to the people there (or their relatives), to find out what the pros and cons of such a move might be.

Of particular concern is the location of the new accommodation. Retirement homes are frequently on the outskirts of cities, and retirement communities can be much further away. In such settings, it can be easy for people to become detached from previous support networks — family, friends, and agencies. A person contemplating such a move should determine his or her willingness and ability to make new friends and contacts, and to enter new professional relationships with doctors, dentists, and so on.

Even more important is the fact that most of the opportunities mentioned involve living in close proximity with other people — sharing in a membership that is making crucial decisions, or perhaps even sharing a room. As it may not be possible to remain detached from one's neighbours, individuals and couples must decide how much they value their privacy.

On the positive side, there are aspects of the new arrangements that can be very appealing. Not everyone enjoys cooking and keeping house, for instance, and some people may look forward to living arrangements in which meals and cleaning are included in the basic cost of the accommodation. Also, circumstances change, and the arrangements which were satisfactory upon retirement may seem less so a decade later. For example, a person's health may decline, or a person who was content to live for years in a house with his or her spouse may feel uncomfortable remaining there after the loss of the spouse. In these situations, the idea of moving into a group home or senior citizens' accommodation may seem not merely acceptable but highly desirable. The new living arrangement could provide the opportunity to meet new people and participate in new activities, to have certain tasks simplified and made easier, as well as the security of knowing that there are people around in case of emergencies. None of these benefits should be taken lightly, and if they happen to fit in with your personality and preferences, then perhaps it is time to consider such a change.

# CHAPTER 4

# Frankly, Doctor...: Your Health During Retirement

*A priest, a minister and a rabbi were having a discussion about the beginning of life. According to the priest, life began at the moment of conception. The minister disagreed. As far as he was concerned, life began at birth. "You're both wrong," the rabbi said. "Life doesn't really begin until the children leave home to marry and the dog dies."*

Anonymous

Just because your middle years are ending and your older ones are beginning doesn't mean that you're over the hill. Thanks to improved living conditions in North America, if you've made it this far, your chances of becoming a member of the geriatric set are excellent. So, consider yourself lucky. With a bit of common sense and sound planning, feel free to enjoy, enjoy, enjoy. As the rabbi put it, life is just beginning.

## A GUIDELINE FOR GOOD HEALTH IN RETIREMENT

To help you preserve your health over the next few decades, I'll provide some guidelines but I'm going to keep away from statistics. Medicine is changing so rapidly that if they were presented, chances are that many would be inaccurate by the time you read them. What I will present instead are ideas and suggestions which you should discuss with your personal health adviser. After all, everyone is different and, hence, diagnosis and treatment of disease has to be individualized. Your own doctor is in the best position to review my recommendations and tailor them to your requirements. Remember that trying to diagnose and treat yourself is a mistake — it requires professional assistance.

### How to Choose a Family Doctor

Naturally, the first step, then, is to choose a physician. Regardless of age, everyone needs a family doctor. You've probably already got one and, if you're like most people, he or she has known you for years. Nonetheless, you might want to make a change, or at least assess the adequacy of your present practitioner. Here's what to look for: First, is your doctor accessible? If you can't get an appointment when you need one, you've got a problem. Most good doctors are busy so it's not unusual to have a week's wait for an appointment, but no matter how booked a doctor is, time should always be reserved for people with urgent problems. If your appendix is about to rupture you can't wait for a week and every doctor knows this. Usually the lack of accessibility isn't the doctor's fault. He or she doesn't book appointments — the receptionist does.

Long before I became a doctor, I learned that it was the secretaries and janitors, not the executives, who ran offices. If you want something from an organization, a good relationship with the little people is oftentimes more important than knowing the big shots. The same holds true in your doctor's office. Get to know the person who answers the phone. She controls access to the doctor.

When you need an urgent appointment, make the fact known to the receptionist. Most doctors trust their office staff to screen calls, or they'd otherwise be talking to a hundred people on the phone and seeing an equal number per day. If you've had to exhaust every strategy you can think of to get by the receptionist, when you finally see the doctor tell him about your frustration.

Doctors usually are sympathetic, but you can't expect miracles — receptionists are harder to replace than patients. Give it another shot and if accessibility doesn't improve, consider one other factor before you begin searching for another doctor: Are you part of the problem? Maybe your personality clashes with the doctor or the office staff. Or, maybe you cry wolf too often and for the wrong reasons. There's not much you can do about a personality clash, but crying wolf is another story altogether. We'll talk about this later.

The next step is to ask yourself whether you feel comfortable with your chosen physician. People who are sick are, by definition, anxious in the doctor's office. They don't know what's wrong and they're worried. Which leads to the fact that many of your symptoms may be the result of personal problems rather than organic diseases. Headache is a good example: maybe your children are responsible instead of a brain tumour.

Needless to say, if you don't feel comfortable with your doctor, he or she won't be able to help you much with your problems. You need a doctor who will listen to you and treat you like a person with symptoms instead of a number with a disease.

You've probably discovered that being older makes you a bit wiser. As the years roll by, extremes become less; black and white fade into grays, and that's the way it should be. If you'll forgive the analogy, your presbyopia (or difficulty trying to read the newspaper without glasses) should make you want to look at all of life more carefully. You don't necessarily have to peer at the world through a magnifying lens, but you should review options before making decisions.

Reviewing medical options can be difficult, however. First you have to know the facts and then you'll have to be briefed on the choices. You might not want the kind of doctor who says: "Morris, you've got cancer. First we'll operate. Next we'll irradiate and then you'll have the benefits of chemotherapy. We'll start on Tuesday. See you then."

You might want to ask questions, such as, what if we don't operate, irradiate or use chemotherapy? There's no law that says you have to agree to being treated to the benefits of modern medicine. You have every right to refuse treatment that you don't want, or demand treatment that isn't being offered to you. Most of all, you have the right to be accurately and fully *informed*.

Choosing a doctor to meet your needs is vital. If you're a questioner, pick someone who will listen and then answer. Shop around until you find someone you get along with on a personal and professional level. In short, find someone you're comfortable with.

It's not that hard for doctors to be competent family physicians. They merely have to be good at two things: first, they have to be able to recognize when you're really sick. When you've got something serious or perhaps life threatening, prompt action has to be taken. This brings us to the second quality of good doctors: they must know what they don't know. In other words, they realize that the ailment from which you're suffering is one that they may not be able to treat effectively, and refer you to a specialist when it's appropriate.

Please don't get confused. Good doctors aren't equivalent to "send me" doctors. Many patients complain that their family doctor continually refers them to specialists, hospitals, laboratories and x-ray facilities. A good doctor won't refer you unless there's a good reason for the referral. And that reason should be explained to you before you agree to accept the decision.

On the other hand, you shouldn't demand to be referred to specialists. The doctor-patient relationship shouldn't be adversarial—you're there to communicate, not argue. After the doctor has given a shot at treating you, a discussion should take place. You might suggest that you're not sure what's wrong with you or ask why the treatment didn't work. After listening to the explanation you're in a position to decide whether or not the family doctor should try another treatment or make a referral. As a rule, doctors don't like to be dictated to, so you might try saying something like: "What about sending me to a specialist? It couldn't hurt, could it?" Be especially wary if your doctor dismisses your complaints or symptoms with the statement: "What can you expect at your age?" Age is not a disease.

If you're looking for a doctor, don't be impressed by initials. M.D., C.M., M.B. stands for medical doctor. C.C.F.P. means Certificant of the College of Family Physicians. Maintaining a C.C.F.P. requires the doctor to put in a number of hours per year in study to help keep him up to date. The same holds true of a doctor who is a Member of the College of Family Physicians (M.C.F.P.). F.R.C.P. means that the doctor is a Fellow of the Royal College of Physicians of Canada. F.R.C.S. is short for a Fellow of the Royal College of Surgeons. Doctors with these initials after their names are medical or surgical specialists. In general you can forget about all the other letters. Some of us with graduate degrees like a master's (M.Sc.) or Ph.D. add the letters to our stationery. I'd like to think that because of our research training we think a bit more critically, but that's merely a personal opinion. It isn't diplomas and initials that make good doctors, so the best way to find a good family physician is by asking friends and relatives for a referral. If they're happy with their doctor, then there's a good chance that you might be happy as well.

## THE INITIAL MEDICAL EXAMINATION
### What a Doctor Should Ask

Once you've lucked into a physician with whom you can communicate and who's accessible, you should then try to assess his or her interest in you. I like to carry out a baseline physical examination on patients, because it gives me an opportunity to know them when they're healthy. A proper examination includes at least some of the following:

First, I want to know who you are. The registration form sitting in front of me will tell me your age, where you were born, where you live, your marital status, religion and your occupation. I begin by expanding on these.

If I don't recognize your address I might ask where the street is or what the neighbourhood is like. This gives me an idea of what resources might be available to help me help you in your part of town. New patients who live a great distance from my offices are often asked to think about whether they really want to become my patient. A family doctor whose office isn't close to your house won't be much use to you if you're bedridden. Many of us will make housecalls on patients who live within walking or reasonable driving distance. I won't, however, travel across the city to see someone and I think it's only fair to tell a patient this at the onset. It's also important to realize that in an emergency an ambulance will take you to the nearest hospital. If you live across town, your family doctor likely won't be visiting or taking care of you because the closest hospital to you probably won't be the one he works out of.

Your marital status is important, because a patient living with a spouse or other person has a valuable resource in case of illness. I like to know what human resources are available to patients who live alone. Are friends nearby? Are there relatives in town? Who do I contact in case of emergency?

If you're separated or divorced, I'm interested in the circumstances and the type of relationship that may still exist. Some people have difficulty adjusting to separation and I consider this important. If your spouse has died, it's also important to know the details and how you've coped.

I'll also want to know about you children and, maybe, even your grandchildren. Some children like to become involved with their parents' health; others don't. There are also parents who don't want their children to know anything about their health. All this is important for me to know in case of emergency or if one of your children happens to telephone.

Your religion is important, because for many patients it's another resource that I may want to utilize at some time in the future. Because the clergy can be an enormous help when serious illness strikes, I'm naturally interested in your relationship with God.

If you're a recent immigrant to Canada, where you were born may be especially useful. It gives me an idea of the standard of health care you've been treated to in the past and may provide some clues if I suspect a disease that isn't native to Canada.

Your occupation is very important for your health assessment because many jobs are associated with hazards. For example, people who work in noisy environments may develop premature hearing problems. Many lung diseases are also related to occupational exposure. Contact with silicon, asbestos, coal dust, beryllium, uranium, iron, tin, antimony, arsenic, barium, cadmium, cement, chromium, coke, mica, vanadium, cotton, flax, hemp, grain and even moldy hay may affect your breathing. Many chemicals including acid fumes, ammonia, cyanides, formaldehyde, hydrogen sulfide, sulfur dioxide and even smoke can damage sensitive lungs. Some of these, along with other chemicals, can put you at more risk of developing cancer. Examples include vinyl chloride, arsenic, petroleum distillates, radio-active compounds and even some drugs like synthetic female and male hormones.

Knowing your occupation also gives me an idea of your level of physical activity and what stresses you've been and are under. If you're still working I might ask how things are going, and whether you enjoy your job. Those patients who are nearing retirement might be asked what plans they've made to fill their time once the day comes when there's no job to go to. And retired people are asked whether or not they're happy with their increased leisure time.

Questions about your present state of mind are very important. An unhappy marriage, job or retirement situation will ultimately bring you to my office complaining of some physical symptom. Let's look at an example: Fred Little, a retired man, has just moved into the city. He's married and lives in an apartment with his 58-year-old wife. He has one son in this city, and other children who live elsewhere. He's got dry, itchy skin which in some places he's scratched to the point where it's bleeding. This problem began three months ago. He tells me that his bowels move irregularly and that he's lost weight. Nine months ago he was admitted to hospital in another city for a thorough bowel examination. It only turned up mild diverticular disease, and in spite of adding fibre to his diet, the bowel problem has persisted.

At this point, I'm thinking cancer. Mr. Little at 67 is the right age, the bowel problem and weight loss are suggestive, and itchy skin could be another symptom.

A physical examination revealed a healthy but thin man who looked his age. Screening blood and urine testing was normal. Six stool samples were tested and found negative for blood. Records from his last doctor showed that his bowel investigation was very thorough and that it was done at a reputable hospital by a respected doctor. A lotion and soap that I prescribed helped the itching.

The next question was whether I should repeat the bowel investigations: barium enema, endoscopy, abdominal CAT scan? The first two tests aren't fun. After discussing my options with Mr. Little, I decided to pass the buck. He was referred to a dermatologist who agreed that although cancer was a possibility, so was my second diagnosis of neurodermatitis (I'll explain later). Next he saw a gastroenterologist (abdominal specialist) who, after satisfying himself that the previous investigation was thorough, suggested that we forget about cancer for the time being.

At a follow-up visit, I met Mrs. Little. The three of us had a long talk and I explained neurodermatitis. In simple terms it meant that his skin was dry and that he scratched it. Could an emotional problem be contributing to the itch? Indeed it could. Tears came to Mrs. Little's eyes.

Neither of them was very happy. Prior to retirement Mr. Little was a workaholic. While the children were growing up he was hardly ever at home. He made no plans for retirement and had no hobbies. His wife took care of the household, paid all the bills, chose the schools and saw to it that the lawn was mowed. The move so they'd be closer to their son was her idea. She was younger and more active than her husband. Her interests included the theatre and pottery, but he had none. At times, the relationship had deteriorated to the point where they discussed divorce. But she was reluctant. Who would take care of him? After all, he was an older man. She couldn't live with what might happen to him if she left.

A referral to a marital therapist was discussed and they both agreed to attend. After a few sessions, the itchy skin bothered him less, his weight increased and his bowels moved more regularly. Our hunch had been right. Taking a family, occupational and marital history paid off.

During a physical examination I will also pursue a personal history, or personal habits that might affect health such as the use of tobacco. Everyone knows that it's related to cancer, heart disease and chronic lung disease. Alcohol use is another habit to be looked into. A drink or two a day probably isn't harmful, but chronic abuse puts a person at risk of a host of disorders including alcoholic liver and heart disease. Alcohol can also damage the brain and nervous system producing memory problems, weakness, numbness and tingling. Because alcoholics have a tendency to eat poorly and smoke too much there are potential risk-related problems. If the patient drinks excessively and works at a dangerous job, or drives, trouble can be expected.

A dietary history may be important. Does my patient eat a balanced diet? Should I be on the look-out for a vitamin deficiency, elevated cholesterol, sugar diabetes or malnutrition?

What about physical exertion? Is regular exercise part of the patient's lifestyle? While I'm not a firm believer that exercise makes a person live longer, I do believe that it makes one feel healthier. It's important to discuss exercise tolerance. We don't want inactive 50-year-old men who sit on their butts all year long out shovelling snow without any warm-up or assurance that they won't be putting themselves at risk. However, immobility and a sedentary life can lead to and exacerbate health problems. Is the patient interested in an activity program? If so, how can I help? If not, why?

Another part of a patient's lifestyle is stress, or, perhaps in better words, wear and tear. We all suffer from both physical and emotional stress. What's important is how much we're under and how much we can take as well as how we deal with it. When you're upset, do you yell and scream, rant and rave, become anxious, depressed, cry, run around the block, or pursue a hobby? The history of your past health is important. A woman without a uterus can't develop uterine cancer. One who's had cancer of the breast needs to be practising regular and meticulous breast self-examination. A history of either type of cancer has significance if I ever decide that female hormones should be prescribed. I'm interested in all serious illnesses, hospitalizations and surgeries a patient has had. Each might have a future significance or put me on the alert as to particular problems I should be looking for. Here are a few examples: Patients with histories of heart or respiratory disease might be offered a shot to prevent pneumonia, and/or yearly flu shots. I might also ask them to telephone or see me quickly whenever they develop a cough or bad cold. Ulcers or stomach problems should make me cautious before I decide to prescribe A.S.A. (Aspirin) or similar drugs.

Next comes the patient's family history. I'm interested in the serious illnesses family members suffered from or died of. In particular, I ask about heart disease, cancer, diabetes, stroke and other disorders which may run in families. Again, this may tip me off with regard to future surveillance and prevention of particular diseases.

Allergies are another concern. I wouldn't want to kill someone by prescribing a drug they're allergic to. Unfortunately, most people really don't know. They might say "penicillin" but when questioned don't really know how they reacted to the drug or what the allergy did. What I'm really interested in are reactions that produce hives, asthma, swelling in the mouth or of the lips, or difficulty in breathing.

Personally, I don't consider allergies to dust, trees, flowers, feathers and the rest of the environment on the same level as drug allergies. I'd like to hear about them under past health. However, anything that's caused hives or breathing problems like bee stings or certain foods is an absolute must for a doctor to know about.

Many people get stomach aches and cramps when they take pills. Sometimes it's the person, sometimes it's the pill. Vague symptoms associated with medications may or may not be significant. If you don't mention them, your doctor will never know.

What about routine immunizations? They're so routine that most adults don't get them. Every one should have a tetanus booster at least every ten years. Polio boosters should be five years apart. The older you are the less likely it is that your shots are up-to-date. Other immunizations aren't routinely necessary except in certain circumstances. For example, if you're around pregnant women and you've never had German measles a shot might be in order if blood tests show that you don't have antibodies. Hepatitis B vaccine should be considered for people who might be exposed to the disease. They include health care workers (especially dentists and those who handle blood and other biological samples), hemopheliacs and people receiving regular blood or blood products, institutionalized people, and homosexuals. Smallpox vaccinations shouldn't be given to anyone routinely. The risk of dying from the vaccination is greater than that of dying from the disease.

Lastly, I'm interested in knowing the names of doctors and hospitals that you've attended, in case I need to request appropriate old medical records from these sources. This causes some people anxiety, especially when they've decided to change family doctors. They're concerned that the old doctor will be angry. If he or she is, it's not your problem. All doctors lose patients, but we all take on new ones. The losses are hopefully balanced by the gains. If they're not, it's our problem, not yours. Most of us have thick skins, so don't be afraid to sign record releases. Don't even be afraid to return to your former doctor if the new one doesn't work out. There is no great shame in trying someone new and then finding that the old doctor was, in fact, better.

Up to this point, all I've done is ask a bunch of questions and observe my patient as he or she responds. Of course, not all the questions are appropriate for each patient, but they should give you an idea of what a doctor might want to know about you, even if you're not sick. With this in mind you might want to think about your responses before consulting a new doctor.

A thorough history involves yet two more areas of inquiry. The first is known as a history of present illness. You should be asked if anything is bothering you at the present time. Depending on your answer, further questions might be asked to hone in on your complaints.

Finally, there's what is called a general functional inquiry. Here you'll be asked a series of questions to determine how your body systems are working. For example: Are you sleeping well? Has your weight remained constant? Has there been any change in the way you move your bowels? Are there any problems when you urinate? For women, what are your menstrual periods like? And for all patients, how's your sex life? There should also be questions about your drug intake. It's important to know which drugs, including vitamins and nonprescription medications, a patient is taking.

## What a Doctor Should Examine

Enough questions. It's time for the actual physical examination. There has been a substantial amount of criticism regarding annual physicals, and many have argued that they're a waste of time and money. In some respects they're right. It isn't necessary to examine every part of a person's body with a microscope every year. Most authorities have suggested partial examinations, the content of which depends on the patient's age. I consider the following examination to be reasonable.

Your weight should be recorded, and your blood pressure checked; I usually do it in both arms. Hearing can be screened for just by noting your responses to change in the volume of my voice during the history taking. The mouth and throat should be looked at. So should your eyes. Ears can be checked for the presence of wax. The thyroid gland which sits below the Adam's apple in the neck should be felt. Your neck, underarms and groin should be examined for bumps or lymph nodes. I listen to the heart and lungs. Breasts are checked in both sexes. I teach women how to examine their own. It should be done once a month, preferably the week after the menstrual period if you're still having one.

In the abdomen I feel for a liver, spleen and masses. The testes and penis are checked and then you should be encouraged to check them yourself once a month. Women should have a pelvic examination which includes a feel of the uterus, tubes and ovaries. Pap smears become less important in middle age. Most authorities suggest that if all your Paps have been normal, repeat tests need only be done every three years. However, women who've had abnormal Pap smears or who are at higher risk of cervical cancer should be checked at least yearly. Risk factors include having lost your virginity at an early age, having had a number of sexual partners and having had genital herpes. Nonetheless, if I'm sticking a speculum into the vagina I'll likely take a Pap smear anyway. It only takes a couple of extra minutes and the cost isn't very high.

All patients should have a rectal examination. Cancer of the bowel is common in both sexes and examination of the prostate through the rectum is a must for all middle-aged males. I look at feet. As a rule they're ignored. Yet deformities such as bunions, hammer toes and callouses can be prevented with the use of proper supports and footwear. And finally, while you're naked I'll be peeking at your skin, looking for cancer.

Some doctors like to run a resting electrocardiogram on their middle-aged and older patients. The rationale is that it's handy to have one on hand to compare with potential future electrocardiograms that might be done if you should start developing chest pain. While this seems reasonable to me, there are doctors who believe it wastes both time and money.

Some doctors also routinely order stress or exercise electrocardiograms on middle-aged people. This test is done while you're jogging on a treadmill. The resting ECG that I mentioned above is useful to pick up disturbances in the electrical conduction of your heart muscle, rhythm problems, and enlargement of the heart, and may show evidence of old heart attacks. The exercise ECG is designed to examine how well your heart works when it's being stressed. Unfortunately, the test isn't perfect; a positive test may not be indicative of an abnormal heart and vice versa, as the following example will show:

A fifty-five-year-old man voiced his concern about his heart to me. He had a brown belt in karate and could beat the pants off me at handball. Still, he was worried about exerting himself. Winter was coming up and he wanted to know if it was safe for him to shovel snow. I agreed to arrange the test. The result indicated that under stress his heart's oxygen supply was less than adequate. He suffered no pain or discomfort while the test was being run and his heart rhythm was normal. I reassured him that he was a "false positive". In other words, I felt the test result was wrong.

Two weeks later he telephoned. Very politely he asked if I would refer him to a cardiologist. As he put it, it wasn't that he didn't trust me, he just wanted to hear the message from a specialist. The cardiologist arranged a Stress Thalium Scan. In this test, a radioactive compound is given, the patient is exercised and the heart is scanned. The images formed give the doctor an idea of how adequate the blood flow is to the heart and how the muscular walls are moving. It's a far more sensitive and specific test than the stress ECG. Thankfully, it was normal. My patient, who is now 61, is still active and hasn't had any heart problems.

Another patient in his fifties went for an annual physical

which included a routine stress ECG. Although he had never
had any symptoms of heart disease, the stress ECG was abnormal.
So was his thalium scan. Coronary catheterization (X-rays done
while dye is being injected into the heart through a tube) showed
that arteries in his heart were clogged. A short time later he had
by-pass surgery. He too is still alive.

Both these examples lead me to believe that routine stress
ECGs shouldn't be performed. The first patient went through
a great deal of anxiety for nothing. The second patient had no
symptoms and risked serious complication during his coronary
catheterization and surgery. The scientific evidence suggesting
that he may now live longer owing to the surgery is controversial.

When it comes to stress ECGs there is no right or wrong
answer. Perhaps they are justified if you've been inactive and
sedentary but now plan to embark on an exercise program. I
feel that doing them on a routine basis isn't justified. Nonetheless, that's my opinion. As I said initially, a lot depends on you
the patient, the circumstances and how your doctor feels. Stress
ECGs are something you should discuss with your own medical
adviser.

Respiratory function or breathing tests may be a good idea
for certain individuals. They can tell you if you're developing
lung or airway disease. I run them on smokers, people with
respiratory problems and anyone whose occupation history
suggests that chest disease might be something I should be looking for. When it comes to smokers, a result showing chronic
obstructive lung disease or early emphysema might be very useful
in convincing the patient to give up the weed. These tests take
only a few minutes and can conveniently be done in the office
as part of a physical.

I like to have baseline blood and urine tests done on all my
middle-aged patients. Normally, the blood is taken after the
person has been fasting for twelve hours. The tests I order include
a complete blood count to give me an idea of what your hemo-
globin is. This will rule out anemia and give me a hint as to
whether your diet is deficient in Vitamin B12 or folic acid.
Screening liver, kidney and thyroid function tests may also be
very helpful. For example, people with drinking problems may
have larger than normal red blood cells or abnormal liver function tests even though they deny drinking alcohol excessively.
An elevated blood uric acid might also indicate a drinking problem or it may suggest that certain modifications to your diet are
necessary. A fasting blood sugar will help to rule out diabetes.

Fasting cholesterol and triglycerides help establish whether your blood fats are elevated enough to require dietary or drug treatment.

From middle age onwards, a simple screening for cancer of the bowel involves analysing stool samples for blood that isn't visible to the eye. The test is easy, inexpensive and can be lifesaving. I recommend it on a yearly basis. Other laboratory tests can be done, but as a rule I don't order them routinely.

Chest X-rays might be in order for certain individuals but I don't believe every patient needs one every year. The same holds true for skin tests to detect tuberculosis. Some doctors believe in a routine or baseline mammogram or breast X-ray for women in the late forties or early fifties. I don't routinely order them, but there is no right or wrong answer. It should be an individual decision based on a particular woman's breasts and her family history of breast cancer.

Measurement of the pressure in your eyes should probably be done. Glaucoma is a major cause of blindness that can usually be prevented or at least delayed if it's caught before permanent damage occurs. Measuring pressures with a Schiotz tonometer is simple and takes only a couple of minutes. Some doctors believe that it's not very accurate while others swear by it. The more accurate measure can be achieved by an ophthalmologist or optometrist using an applanation tonometer, but they'd be overburdened if everyone over the age of 45 attended for an annual exam. The Schiotz measurement which your family doctor can do is probably good enough as a screening test for people with healthy eyes and no family history of glaucoma. Those with a family history or eye problems can have applanation tonometry done during routine visits to their eye specialist.

## HOW YOU CAN KEEP YOURSELF HEALTHY IN RETIREMENT

Assuming that all the history taking and the physical examination don't suggest areas for further inquiry or investigation, you should now be interested in keeping yourself healthy. Here are a few suggestions:

### Keep Active

Don't let the child in you grow up. If you do, you'll get old. Jump over puddles. Play kick-the-can. Walk up stairs. Exercise will keep your heart, circulatory system, muscles, joints and lungs tuned up. You may not live longer, but you'll sure feel much better.

Those of you who've been sedentary should consult your doctor before embarking on an exercise program. The safest way to become involved is to join a fitness club that offers well-supervised programs. It's not wise to start without expert advice. You need to be taught what you can and can't or shouldn't do, and how to warm up and cool down before and after exercising.

If you must start on your own, try walking. Do it with a partner, and progress to brisk walking. Swimming and bicycling are also popular. So are dancing and golf. Watch your level of exertion. Avoid sudden bursts of exertion that may put undue stress on your heart and lungs.

## Watch Your Eating Habits

You don't have to be poor to be malnourished. Nor does good nutrition have to be related to socioeconomic status. We eat for a number of reasons. One is to provide our bodies with energy. Another is to satiate ourselves. For many people, eating is fun and associated with social functions. That's why many elderly people who live alone eat poorly and must be careful that they are getting a balanced diet. Normal changes in the sensory functions of taste and smell can also affect appetites in the elderly and ways must be found to compensate for these changes so that their enjoyment of food will not lessen.

If you want to ensure that you're receiving adequate protein, carbohydrate, fat and vitamins, follow Canada's Food Rules. Personal experience, however, dictates that few people strictly adhere to these or many other government edicts. Instead, most Canadians tend to overdo it. Our diets are rich in carbohydrates and fat. The usual feedback I get from patients who've been referred to dietitians is: "What the hell does that skinny kid know? I love food. If I've got to eat gruel for the rest of my life, I'd rather be dead."

Common sense dictates that moderation is the key. Cut down on portions. Avoid refined carbohydrates whenever possible. These include sugar and honey. Complex carbohydrates like grains, cereals, beans and vegetables are preferable. Protein can come from fish, fowl, meat, dairy and vegetable sources. Dairy products are important for their calcium content as well as protein. All of us lose calcium from our bones as we age, which puts us at risk of fractures. After menopause, women are especially susceptible. Some doctors feel the problem is significant enough to routinely recommend calcium supplementation.

Fat in the diet is a controversial subject. Many people equate cholesterol with poison, and avoid eggs, butter and red meats. The best I can say, at time of writing, is that all the answers aren't in yet. Blood cholesterol has been subdivided into HDL or high-density cholesterol and LDL or low-density. When it comes to cholesterol and heart disease, the significant number is the ratio between HDL and total blood cholesterol. The ideal situation is to have a high HDL and a low total cholesterol. HDL can be increased by exercise and the consumption of one or two drinks of alcohol per day. Total cholesterol can be reduced by watching dietary intake. One recent study suggested that lowering cholesterol intake and/or lowering blood levels with the use of drugs prevents heart attacks. The implication is that people should have their blood fats measured and dietary and drug treatments implemented as required.

The whole area of blood fat and cholesterol will be a hotly debated one in the years to come. Therefore, I won't take a stand one way or the other. Again, common sense dictates moderation. Animal fat intake should be carefully monitored as should your intake of other saturated fats. Unsaturated fats such as those found in sunflower, safflower, corn and soybean should be substituted. I'd suggest that you discuss this topic with your doctor rather than rely on books and articles which may well be outdated by the time you read them.

Salt or sodium chloride has also been equated with poison by some people. But both sodium and chloride are essential to life. Once again, the answer is moderation. Your salt requirement can be met by eating unsalted food, so there's no reason to salt or oversalt anything. We'd all likely be much better off if the salt shaker had never been invented.

Another hot topic is fibre. Food that used to be thrown away or fed to animals is now in vogue for people. Fibre or roughage isn't absorbed by the body and, based on the fact that anything that passed from mouth to toilet without giving up nutrients was waste, most processed food was formulated to be low in fibre. This led to diets that were low in bulk. The trouble is, bulk makes our bowels move and regular bowel movements are important.

In comparison to native Africans, most Westernized people are constipated. Yet, by our standards, most citizens in the Third

World who aren't starving suffer from diarrhea. What's important is not *how often* you evacuate so much as *how long* it takes food to pass from mouth to toilet. This is known as transit time. The chief oracle of the fibre hypothesis was Burkitt. He concluded that the natives had healthier bowels than Westerners. They have fewer hemorrhoids, varicose veins, diverticular disease, cancer of the colon, gallstones and other gut-related problems.

Research showed that Ugandan villagers eating natural foods put out an average of 470 grams of stool per day with a transit time of 36 hours, while British seaman only managed to produce 104 grams on average with a transit time averaging 83 hours. In terms of fibre, the Africans consumed 60 grams per day as compared to the British who consumed a meagre 12 grams.

Basically, the fibre supporters argue that man cannot live on nutrients alone. However, it's less than scientific to make comparisons between the fibre found in African fruits and vegetables versus those found in bran. We do know, however, that fibre will increase fecal bulk and reduce transit time. It produces a softer stool and a more regular bowel movement. Because fibre may increase the solubility of cholesterol in the gallbladder, it might, therefore, prevent cholesterol gallstone formation. Some types of fibres may reduce serum cholesterol and triglycerides. Fibre reduces or slows carbohydrate absorption. In diabetics a high fibre diet may improve sugar tolerance and reduce the need for insulin and other sugar-lowering drugs. Fibre is filling and may therefore eliminate the need to eat foods containing excess carbohydrates and fat.

I'll leave the decision to you and your doctor as to whether you should become a fibre convert. Coarse bran is cheap and a heaping tablespoon contains 2.4 grams of fibre. A 100-gram bowl of All Bran cereal contains 26.7 grams of fibre. By most accounts you need at least 20 grams of fibre per day to balance your diet.

## Vitamins and Minerals

What about vitamins? If you eat reasonably, you don't need them. The possible exception is the post-menopausal woman with osteoporosis or excessive calcium loss from her bones. As mentioned, some doctors recommend calcium supplements for these women sometimes in combination with Vitamin D supplements.

Taking a multiple vitamin every day plus some Vitamin C and Vitamin E won't hurt you, but on the other hand it likely won't help you. Because the B Complex vitamins and Vitamin C don't accumulate in your body, you'll excrete whatever you don't need. However, fat-soluble vitamins like A and D can be very dangerous if taken in excessive quantities. While many testimonials exist proclaiming miracle cures with the use of mega or high-dose vitamins, scientific proof is all but lacking. Don't partake in vitamin popping without your doctor's knowledge.

The same holds true for minerals. For example, iron deficiency in a middle-aged or older person must be equated with blood loss. No one should simply take iron supplements to maintain an iron balance. It's absolutely essential that your doctor determine where the loss of blood is coming from in your body. It might be excessive menstrual loss. Or it could be from a silent ulcer or a cancer in your colon.

Unfortunately, as people reach the age of 45 they start to worry about their mortality. This makes them susceptible to cons by health food freaks and vitamin pushers. Don't get sucked in. Hair analysis has no proven benefit, and expensive vitamins likely don't work any better than the cheaper ones you can buy at the drugstore. Use your head. Vitamin C is Vitamin C whether it comes from clover or a test tube.

## Sex — It's Good For You

Next comes sex. Have it. It's fun. Enjoy. Do whatever makes you feel good. Fantasize. Sex is simply a form of communication. If you're having difficulties, it's likely that the problem originates in your communications centre and not in your genitals.

Just because *Playboy* and *Playgirl* don't publish pictures of nude fifty-year-olds doesn't mean that the middle-aged body isn't sexy. Regardless of age, you can enjoy a sexual relationship. Sure your needs may be different and you might enjoy new forms of lovemaking. It's not unusual for things to change over time.

Sexual drive is not lost when menopause begins. Menstruation has nothing to do with being a sexual being. Some women find that their vaginas lubricate less after menopause, which can lead to painful intercourse. Don't suffer; tell your doctor. Estrogen pills or creams will cure you. Or if they're not appropriate, a simple lubricant like KY Jelly may do the trick. The same holds true if you've had a hysterectomy or a mastectomy. It needn't affect your sexuality.

Think of menopause as a blessing — you'll never have to worry about your "friend" arriving unexpectedly. Menopause simply means that your ovaries are no longer responding and producing estrogen. It's no big deal. Most women can receive estrogen replacement in pill form. Again, this is a controversial area.

Personally, I'm a believer in hormone replacement. Not only will it prevent hot flashes and a dry vagina, but if started early, estrogen prevents some of the calcium loss from your bones. Some doctors disagree. There's a lingering fear that estrogen contributes to cancer of the uterus. It's a complex argument that you should discuss with your personal physician. To counteract the estrogen effect and its cancer-producing potential, many doctors cycle the hormones. I prescribe natural estrogen from the first to the twenty-fifth day of each month and add progesterone from days sixteen to twenty-five. From the twenty-sixth to the end of the month, my patients don't take any hormones.

What I've gleaned from the medical literature is that the risks of developing uterine cancer with estrogen are far less than those of fracturing a hip because of osteoporosis. When you add progesterone to the regime, the chances of developing cancer of the uterus may in fact be less than if no hormones were prescribed at all. And the estrogen still prevents calcium loss from your bones. Naturally, certain women (for example, those who have had breast cancer) shouldn't take estrogen. For these reasons, a long discussion with your doctor is in order. And who knows, by the time you reach menopause, a better hormone replacement regime may be available.

Women who can't take or aren't prescribed estrogen still need not suffer through menopausal symptoms. Various drugs are available to counteract hot flashes. Go see your doctor.

Back to men. As you get older, your prostate may well get larger. Symptoms include waking at night to urinate, less power when you urinate and dribbling when you're done. Not to worry. Most prostatic enlargement is benign, not cancerous. Every male should have a yearly rectal examination to assess the size and consistency of the prostate. And if yours is enlarged and surgery is recommended, stop worrying. It is unusual for prostatic surgery to affect your ability to perform.

Impotence, trouble getting it up, difficulty keeping it hard, or whatever, isn't uncommon. Often the problem is fear of failure. Insecurity about your relationship or your masculine image can be another cause. Another difficulty comes when you try to will an erection. It's like lying in bed repeating sleep, sleep, sleep when you can't fall asleep. The more you repeat sleep, the more frustrated and less likely you are to fall asleep. The best way to achieve an erection is to forget about achieving an erection. Relax. Get in the mood, with lots of foreplay. Nature will take care of the erection.

If it doesn't, discuss your problem with your spouse, and consult your doctor. There are legitimate causes for erectile failure. Drugs are one of the most common causes and some of the medications used to treat high blood pressure are notorious for this effect. Some doctors are prudish and won't ask about drug side effects that are sexual in nature. Don't let your doctor's hang-up affect your sex life. Lay the cards on the table. It's almost always possible to switch to drugs which allow good blood pressure control and a powerful erection. Some diseases like diabetes or arteriosclerosis may be the problem. You'll never know if you don't ask. One question your doctor should ask is whether you ever wake with a spontaneous erection. During dream sleep erections are common, and many men wake with an erection in the morning. If you have an erection while sleeping or in the morning, in all likelihood your problem is psychological, not physical. And if you don't know about the changing posture of your penis during sleep, it's possible for you to spend the night in a sleep lab where it can be measured while you slumber.

Another common cause of sexual dysfunction is heart disease. Anyone who's had a heart attack is scared of having another heart attack. The same holds true for other major physical illnesses. Discuss your fears with your doctor. In all likelihood you'll be reassured and told to enjoy and stop worrying. Many of us do suggest one caution. Stick to lovemaking with your wife. A mistress can be dangerous. Maybe it's the guilt, or because mistresses could be more psychologically exciting. If you suffer from angina and sex causes attacks, mention it to your doctor. Nitro can be used for more than helping you climb stairs pain-free. A nitroglycerine tablet before sex can be very effective.

Some men seek or rely on drugs to alter the anatomy of their penises. Vitamin E is a common choice. Personally, I've seen no convincing evidence about its benefits, but who cares. If it makes you function, use it.

A prescription drug that some men swear by is yohimbine. It's been around as long as mankind. Testosterone has also been used. It's probable that drug therapy simply fools your brain into forgetting about the size of your penis and without the brain's input nature takes over. Presto, you've got an erection. Few males are actually testosterone deficient and, if used for prolonged periods of time at high doses, this hormone can be dangerous.

Whether you're male or female, if sex is a problem talk to your family doctor. If physical causes have been ruled out and counselling is in order, ask for a referral to a sexual therapist, if your doctor can't help you. And like I said, relax. An experienced therapist can teach any couple to enjoy.

## MAINTAINING GOOD HEALTH IN RETIREMENT

Many people wonder how often they should go to their doctor for maintenance check-ups. I'm still a believer in a yearly once-over. It needn't be as exhaustive as the initial encounter that I described previously. However, the areas discussed should be updated and an appropriate physical examination and laboratory assessment are in order.

When it comes to trouble-shooting, if you opt to diagnose and treat yourself it's at your own risk. Like the "good" doctor, a smart patient can help him/herself so long as he/she knows what he/she doesn't know. If you're convinced that all you've got is a cold, then there's no reason to see your doctor. A run-of-the-mill headache is not an indication for a neurological consultation and CAT scan. Occasional indigestion which is relieved by antacids doesn't necessitate an X-ray of the stomach.

Use your judgement. Something that's getting better or goes away on its own probably isn't serious. If it persists, recurs or gets worse, you should worry and see your doctor. When you're not sure, err on the side of caution, and make an appointment.

Should you choose self-medication, please remember that the local pharmacist knows a lot more than how to count pills and label bottles. He or she is a resource person. Introduce yourself and establish a relationship. Discuss your choice of non-prescription medication before you make any purchase. Don't forget to mention your diet, amount of activity, allergies, other medical conditions that you might have, and the fact that you're also taking other drugs. Ask for advice about consulting your physician.

Never rely on advertising when you are choosing a non-prescription medicine. Most advertising is misleading. Anything that you put in your mouth, up your rectum, in your vagina or on your skin can be potentially dangerous.

Keep away from nose sprays, decongestant eye drops and laxatives. You can get hooked on them all. You'd better see a doctor if you're a regular aspirin or painkiller taker. Something must be wrong if you need all those pills. And don't use pills prescribed for someone else—just because they work for them doesn't mean they'll be good for you.

## PHYSIOLOGICAL CHANGES IN THE AGING PROCESS

There are some physiological changes in aging which are bound to occur. I'm going to list them but don't get the idea that all of them will happen to you—some of them, perhaps, but not necessarily all. The set of genes you inherited from your parents and the care you take of your health will determine the extent of the following changes common to the elderly.

### Posture and Gait:

There can be a forward bowing of the spine or flexing of the knees and hip which will change your posture. Your stature may also decrease as well as the length of your stride and the height of your steps.

### Skin:

The changes in this organ are often the most noticeable sign of aging as it becomes less elastic, thinner and more wrinkled. Itching can become a problem due to too frequent washing of the drier and more sensitive skin. There is also a decline in the number of sweat glands which can cause a decrease in the body's ability to sweat and to conserve heat.

### Hair:

There is a change in the distribution, pigmentation and texture of body hair with a tendency in males toward baldness and increased hair on the body and in the ears and nose. Females have a tendency to develop coarse facial hair.

### Cardiovascular System:

The heart's efficiency as a pump is decreased, particularly under stressful conditions, and the strength of the heart muscle's contraction is reduced. The arteries become more rigid which can cause a rise in blood pressure, and the receptors in the aorta which are responsible for adjusting the blood pressure during changes in posture become less efficient. Everyone knows that high blood pressure can cause strokes but just what constitutes high blood pressure in older people remains a controversial issue as it is difficult to know whether raised blood pressure is a normal aspect of aging or a disease to be treated. Physicians in the United States adopt an aggressive approach in this regard and recommend treatment while in the United Kingdom a more conservative approach is taken by many geriatricians. In Canada, doctors are taking a mid-position between the two differing practices until more definite evidence is available.

## Respiratory System:

Although there is a loss of lung tissue elasticity and the lungs are less efficient in expelling air, these changes shouldn't impede the aged from taking part in normal activities.

## Gastrointestinal System:

A slowed motility of the gastrointestinal tract and a reduction in the blood supply which leads to a slight decline in the intestines' absorptive capability could cause constipation if the elderly person has a poor diet and little exercise combined with the abuse of laxatives.

## Renal System:

The aging kidney decreases in ability to excrete waste products as well as to dilute urine. The bladder wall may become unstable and contract at an earlier stage of filling which causes a more frequent urge to pass urine.

## Musculoskeletal Changes:

Progressive changes take place in the proportions of the body's components—muscle bulk diminishes while the amount of fat increases. Bone loss of the spine can cause curvature with a resulting loss of height. Both muscle and bone loss can be diminished by continued regular exercise and good nutrition, particularly if maintained from early adulthood.

## Sleep:

A change in sleep habit or the inability to get restful sleep is a common complaint among older individuals. Older persons spend a longer time falling asleep, have less sleep associated with dreams, less deep sleep and wake more frequently during the night. However, they spend approximately the same amount of time asleep in a given 24-hour period as a younger person, if daytime naps are taken into account. Accepting this changed pattern of sleep will work much better than attempting to achieve the pattern of sleep associated with your youth.

Sleeping pills have only a short-lived benefit and have definite side effects. In many cases, they further disturb the sleep pattern and cause a rebound sleeplessness when stopped. They may also cause a hangover effect with light-headedness, weakness or drowsiness the next day. A warm drink or a small amount of alcohol, combined with regular daytime activity, can be more effective. You should remember that alcohol in larger quantities paradoxically irritates the brain and disrupts sleep patterns.

## Aging of the Eye:

At about the ages of 45 to 55 many people begin to require glasses and better lighting for close work. This gradual deterioration of vision may be attributed to decreased elasticity of the lens in the eye. Vision in later years may also be impaired by diseases such as senile macular-degeneration where central vision is lost but peripheral vision remains. Senile cataracts—lens opacities—commonly develop and obstruct normal vision. Surgical intervention by removal of the cataract can readily remedy this latter condition. Glaucoma, another common condition which is due to the obstruction of the drainage of fluid from the eye, can lead to blindness if appropriate early treatment is neglected.

## Hearing Changes:

The major manifestations of progressive hearing loss involve the inability to hear the higher frequency sounds, and a loss of discrimination which leads to rapid speech sounding garbled and unintelligible. Environmental factors are known to play a role since there is much less hearing loss in rural rather than urban areas.

Diseases which also cause deafness in the elderly include otosclerosis, a progressive disease involving the middle ear; inflammatory diseases of the ears; and damage due to some drugs. However, in many cases, hearing loss in the elderly turns out to be nothing alarming—simply a buildup of cerumen or wax in the ear canals.

## WARNING SIGNS AND SYMPTOMS

There are certain warning signs and symptoms that should prompt you to see your doctor. Let's start with the head and work down:

A headache that's different from any kind you've had before. If it's the worst headache you've ever had in your life, or when it's associated with a stiff neck. If along with the headache there are other neurological symptoms such as numbness, tingling, weakness, or visual disturbance. Or if your usual cure for a run-of-the-mill headache doesn't work.

Memory changes. Difficulty remembering recent events. Sleeping problems, such as difficulty falling asleep, or waking early in the morning. Crying for no reason. Loss of drive and ambition. Just simply feeling like you don't care about anything. Strange feelings. Hearing voices. Excessive anxiety. Tremors.

Changes in visual acuity. Pain in your eyes. The sudden development of an aversion to light. Seeing halos around lights at night.

Recurrent nosebleeds. Chronic breathing difficulty. Pain or discharge in your ears. Sudden episodes of dizziness or light-headedness.

Any growths or ulcers in your mouth. Bleeding gums. Changes in the lines or size of your tongue.

Lumps or bumps in your neck, armpits or groin area. Any new skin rash. A change in the shape, pigmentation or size of an existing mole on your skin. Anything on your skin that starts to bleed, doesn't seem to be healing or appears to be growing larger.

Naturally, you'll be examining your breasts every month. Your doctor will have taught you how, right? If you have menstrual periods, you'll be doing it during the week following your period. If not, you'll do it the first day of each month. If during your examination a new lump or mass turns up, you'll go to the phone and dial doctor.

A cough that won't go away. A productive cough with blood-tinged sputum. Sudden development of shortness of breath.

Chest, neck, jaw or arm pain that occurs with exertion and goes away when you rest. Any severe chest, neck, jaw or arm pain whether related to exertion or not, especially if associated with shortness of breath, palpitations (funny heart beats) and/or sweats. Recurrent palpitations, especially if associated with weakness or dizziness.

Recurrent indigestion. Indigestion that's not relieved by antacids within a reasonable period of time. Recurrent vomiting. Vomit containing blood. Recurrent abdominal pain. Abdominal pain that radiates to the right shoulder (it may be your gallbladder). Increased appetite. Loss of appetite. Weight loss that can't be explained by a diet. Any change in bowel habits. Blood in your stool, in the toilet or on the toilet tissue. Black stool that looks like road tar. Never, ever assume that blood in your stool is from hemorrhoids. You're in the cancer age group. All rectal bleeding must be diagnosed by a professional and never treated routinely as the TV commercials suggest.

Trouble urinating. A change in your pattern of urination. Need to get up at night to urinate. Decreased urinary flow. Dribbling when you've finished. Increased urinary frequency. Loss of urine when you cough or laugh. Blood in your urine. Pain with urination. Increased thirst.

Any menstrual irregularity: increased frequency, decreased frequency, increased flow, decreased flow, changes in menstrual cramping. If you're menopausal and not on hormones, any menstrual bleeding should be reported. If you're on cyclical hormones some bleeding may be acceptable during your hormone-free days; nonetheless it should be reported. An absolute must is the reporting of any bleeding on days when you're taking your hormone pills.

Vaginal discharge. A change in the pigmentation of your external genitalia. Pain at penetration, during or after intercourse. Bleeding associated with intercourse.

Joint swelling or redness, which in conjunction with pain, means arthritis. If there is pain alone, it's arthralgia. Arthritis should be reported, but with arthralgia you can wait to see if it goes away by itself.

Naturally, I can't be exhaustive or entirely complete. But remember what I said initially; if you're worried about anything, see a doctor. Worry alone is good enough reason.

# DEALING WITH CHRONIC MEDICAL PROBLEMS

Those of you with medical problems should remember that although medicine has come a long way in a very short period of time, we still have much more to learn. Much of the brain still remains a mystery. The causes of many diseases are still unknown. There are a host of maladies for which effective therapy has yet to be discovered. In short, medicine isn't perfect and doctors aren't gods.

Because some diseases such as hypertension and glaucoma don't have symptoms, they're awfully hard to accept. For example, you go to the doctor for a routine examination. You're feeling great, but the doctor drops a bomb. You discover you're sick, and have to take pills or eyedrops.

Most doctors handle their dismayed patients fairly well. They know that no person in his right mind is going to take medication for the rest of his life for a symptomless disease he doesn't understand. They, therefore, explain that your elevated blood pressure could lead to premature heart attack, stroke, blindness or kidney disease. Or that the elevated pressure in your eyes might lead to blindness. Without this understanding, the odds are you won't take the medication.

And the treatment has to be explained to the patient as well. In the case of high blood pressure, lifestyle modification should be discussed. Limiting salt intake, weight reduction and exercise are important. The patient should also know that any drug has potential side effects. There are ways to help you remember to take your medications. For example, compartmentalized pill containers which hold a day's worth of medication are available. The treatment should be streamlined, because the fewer the pills you have to take, the more likely you'll be to take them. A good doctor will keep your medications to a minimum.

Some diagnoses are quite meaningless. Arthritis means pain, swelling, redness and heat in a joint or joints, but there are many causes for arthritis. Infection is one, and it can be cured with antibiotics. More commonly, however, arthritis can't be cured and the best you can expect is effective treatment for symptom relief. Even so, there's arthritis and arthritis. Degenerative or osteoarthritis means that wear and tear in the joints is causing the problems. Rheumatoid or systemic lupus erythematosis are but two examples of other types of arthritis. And even within the types there are variations. One person may be crippled by rheumatoid arthritis while another can effectively be treated with the occasional Aspirin.

All drugs used in the treatment of non-infective arthritis have the potential to produce side effects, the most common of which is stomach upset. You need to discuss these side effects with your doctor. For some patients physio and/or occupational therapy may be helpful, while appliances like joint splints, canes, walkers and even wheelchairs might be necessary for some affected people. Remember that complex disorders have complicated and multifaceted treatments.

Most chronic diseases are also represented by "disease clubs" in which patients with the disease have gotten together to help themselves. Some of these self-help groups have evolved into multi-million-dollar organizations that provide volunteers, hold meetings, lobby governments and raise money for research and their members' needs. They can be of tremendous assistance. If you've got a chronic disease, ask around about disease clubs. Check the telephone book, ask your doctor, the public health nurse or your local hospital. The clubs usually have a public information officer who will answer your questions and who might even refer you to a specialist if you feel that your own doctor doesn't know what he/she is doing. They're also handy for checking out quack or unproven "cures".

Finally, as I mentioned earlier in the chapter, people with chronic diseases can get depressed. It's natural—few sane people want to be sick. Be on the lookout for depression, and try to spot it early. The symptoms are a change in personality, increased anxiety, frustration, loss of appetite, trouble sleeping, loss of interest in life, difficulty concentrating, and even thoughts about suicide. Everyone with a chronic illness needs human support, so we're back to square one. Chronic disease or not, everyone, regardless of age, needs caring relationships, one of which should be with a family physician. Sometimes the concern of another human being is worth more than any medicine or surgical therapy. When it comes to chronic disease it may be all that a doctor really has to offer. Don't forget to remind yours of the fact.

## A HEALTH CHECKLIST FOR THE RETIRED

To conclude this chapter, here's a summary of what's been advised for older people who want to stay healthy so they can enjoy life:

1. Find a family doctor
2. Attend for a full physical
3. Pay attention to communications in all interpersonal relationships
4. Keep active
5. Use common sense when you eat
6. Don't waste money on vitamins
7. Attend to your sexual needs
8. Plan for your retirement
9. Know your limitations when you trouble-shoot
10. Don't rely on drugs
11. Call your doctor when you're worried about your health
12. Visit your doctor for periodic maintenance
13. Make sure that you understand treatment plans and follow them
14. Utilize community resources including disease clubs
15. Remember that the mind and body are inseparable. Health is both mental and physical

and lastly, A Gram of Prevention Is Worth A Kilogram Of Cure.

# CHAPTER 5

# Taking It With You: Financial Planning for Retirement

*Old age takes away from us what we have inherited and gives us what we have earned.*

Gerald Brenan
*Thoughts in a Dry Season* (1978)

Philosophically, there is some comfort in Brenan's observation. Practically, there is no comfort at all unless your old age is planned for in good time. Until fairly recently, the notion of retirement was almost unheard of. People worked for as long as they could, withdrawing from the workforce only when health or other factors made it necessary. The concept of retirement planning was also generally unknown, and a person who left his job usually became the charge of his family or of society as a whole.

Happily, all this has changed. Retirement is now accepted as the norm, and the vast majority of people look forward to retirement as a time, good health permitting, in which to pursue activities which the constraints of work made impossible. Of course, the pursuit of many activities requires a financial base for support after one's salary or business income has ceased. Canadians are fortunate in that they have a well-developed public pension system which will give at least a minimum standard of living to all residents. Further, for a very large number of employees the private sector now provides pension plans which should produce an additional source of income linked to what they have earned during their years with their employers. In cases where the pension may be modest or non-existent, the income-tax system provides an opportunity for you to provide your own pension which is funded in part by your contributions and in part through "tax concessions". Finally, unless you are in a position where you need every dollar you earn to live on, you should be able to build up an asset base of personal investments which will be available to draw upon when you need it to make your retirement years comfortable.

But when you are planning for retirement, you should also be considering the unforeseen. What happens if you die before retirement, leaving people behind who were dependent upon you? What happens if you are disabled and are unable to work? How can you best meet your continuing obligations to your family and still ensure that you will have enough money to live comfortably?

In this chapter we shall be examining these various issues. In the next chapter, we shall be looking at what has come to be known as "estate planning", essentially those techniques that, used now, guarantee that when you die your dependents will be taken care of in the manner you would like.

By definition, any broad discussion of financial planning or estate planning will iclude a significant component of tax planning. There are many tax provisions which are designed to facilitate both retirement planning and estate planning. And there are techniques available which will allow you to minimize taxes while you are still working. These latter are important because the key to building an "estate" is by building a capital base, a fund of money or other assets which are yours, free and clear, after all taxes have been paid. Ensuring that you pay the least possible amount of tax while you are earning your income will help to build a greater capital base for your retirement, which will be added protection for both you and your family.

## WHEN SHOULD FINANCIAL PLANNING FOR RETIREMENT START?

Generally speaking, a person's financial life follows a pattern. In the early years, most of one's income goes towards meeting current needs and building up "basic assets", such as acquiring a home, furniture, automobiles, and the like. During the next stage of working life, a very considerable portion of your income will go to the support and education of your children. But then, the children grow up and the house is paid for, and the time comes to start thinking of accumulating assets, such as a portfolio of stocks and bonds. Many people do not seriously start to contemplate saving for retirement until they reach their fifties. This attitude towards retirement saving is quite understandable. It is extremely difficult, when you are 25, to set aside, say, $1,000 for your retirement when there are so many other demands upon your income.

Yet it is quite clear that $1,000 set aside for retirement at age 25 is worth a lot more than $1,000 set aside for retirement at age 50. This is because the most commonly used retirement plans are "tax-sheltered", which means that the income generated is not taxed each year (as investment income in your own hand is taxed). Instead the income is compounded on a tax-free basis until it is withdrawn from the plan.

Suppose that at age 25 you put $1,000 into a registered retirement savings plan (known generally as an RRSP) and the plan pays 10 per cent per year. If you were to retire at age 65, the value of the $1,000 would have grown to about $45,260. If you put the same $1,000 in the plan when you were 50, so that it would compound tax free for just 15 years, the amount you could withdraw would be just $4,177. (If you had invested the $1,000 personally and paid tax at 50 per cent per year on the income, at the end of 40 years you would have $7,040 and at the end of 15 years, $2,079!)

The point is obvious. When you consider retirement planning, especially if a tax-sheltered plan is to be used, the earlier you start the better off you are. And while it is never too late to start planning for retirement, the rule of thumb is that the earlier the better; a dollar invested at an early age is worth much more than a dollar invested later.

The following Table A shows how $100 will accumulate when

invested at various rates of interest. For example, $100 at 10% will accumulate to $1,083 after 25 years.

## TABLE A

| YEAR | I = 7.5% | I = 10% | I = 12.5% | I = 15% |
|------|----------|---------|-----------|---------|
| 1 | 108 | 110 | 113 | 115 |
| 2 | 116 | 121 | 127 | 132 |
| 3 | 124 | 133 | 142 | 152 |
| 4 | 134 | 146 | 160 | 175 |
| 5 | 144 | 161 | 180 | 201 |
| 6 | 154 | 177 | 203 | 231 |
| 7 | 166 | 195 | 228 | 266 |
| 8 | 178 | 214 | 257 | 306 |
| 9 | 192 | 236 | 289 | 352 |
| 10 | 206 | 259 | 325 | 405 |
| 11 | 222 | 285 | 365 | 465 |
| 12 | 238 | 314 | 411 | 535 |
| 13 | 256 | 345 | 462 | 615 |
| 14 | 275 | 380 | 520 | 708 |
| 15 | 296 | 418 | 585 | 814 |
| 16 | 318 | 459 | 658 | 936 |
| 17 | 342 | 505 | 741 | 1076 |
| 18 | 368 | 556 | 833 | 1238 |
| 19 | 395 | 612 | 937 | 1423 |
| 20 | 425 | 673 | 1055 | 1637 |
| 21 | 457 | 740 | 1186 | 1882 |
| 22 | 491 | 814 | 1335 | 2164 |
| 23 | 528 | 895 | 1501 | 2489 |
| 24 | 567 | 985 | 1689 | 2863 |
| 25 | 610 | 1083 | 1900 | 3292 |
| 26 | 656 | 1192 | 2138 | 3786 |
| 27 | 705 | 1311 | 2405 | 4354 |
| 28 | 758 | 1442 | 2706 | 5007 |
| 29 | 814 | 1586 | 3044 | 5758 |
| 30 | 875 | 1745 | 3424 | 6621 |
| 31 | 941 | 1919 | 3852 | 7614 |
| 32 | 1012 | 2111 | 4334 | 8757 |
| 33 | 1088 | 2323 | 4876 | 10070 |
| 34 | 1169 | 2555 | 5485 | 11580 |
| 35 | 1257 | 2810 | 6171 | 13318 |
| 36 | 1351 | 3091 | 6942 | 15315 |
| 37 | 1452 | 3400 | 7810 | 17612 |
| 38 | 1561 | 3740 | 8786 | 20254 |
| 39 | 1679 | 4114 | 9884 | 23292 |
| 40 | 1804 | 4526 | 11120 | 26786 |

## TABLE B

| YEAR | I = 7.5% | I = 10% | I = 12.5% | I = 15% |
|------|----------|---------|-----------|---------|
| 1 | 108 | 110 | 113 | 115 |
| 2 | 223 | 231 | 239 | 247 |
| 3 | 347 | 364 | 381 | 399 |
| 4 | 481 | 511 | 542 | 574 |
| 5 | 624 | 672 | 722 | 775 |
| 6 | 779 | 849 | 925 | 1007 |
| 7 | 945 | 1044 | 1153 | 1273 |
| 8 | 1123 | 1258 | 1409 | 1579 |
| 9 | 1315 | 1494 | 1698 | 1930 |
| 10 | 1521 | 1753 | 2023 | 2335 |
| 11 | 1742 | 2038 | 2388 | 2800 |
| 12 | 1981 | 2352 | 2799 | 3335 |
| 13 | 2237 | 2697 | 3261 | 3950 |
| 14 | 2512 | 3077 | 3781 | 4658 |
| 15 | 2808 | 3495 | 4367 | 5472 |
| 16 | 3126 | 3954 | 5025 | 6408 |
| 17 | 3468 | 4460 | 5766 | 7484 |
| 18 | 3835 | 5016 | 6599 | 8721 |
| 19 | 4230 | 5627 | 7536 | 10144 |
| 20 | 4655 | 6300 | 8591 | 11781 |
| 21 | 5112 | 7040 | 9777 | 13663 |
| 22 | 5603 | 7854 | 11112 | 15828 |
| 23 | 6130 | 8750 | 12613 | 18317 |
| 24 | 6698 | 9735 | 14302 | 21179 |
| 25 | 7308 | 10818 | 16202 | 24471 |
| 26 | 7963 | 12010 | 18340 | 28257 |
| 27 | 8668 | 13321 | 20745 | 32610 |
| 28 | 9426 | 14763 | 23451 | 37617 |
| 29 | 10240 | 16349 | 26495 | 43375 |
| 30 | 11115 | 18094 | 29919 | 49996 |
| 31 | 12057 | 20014 | 33771 | 57610 |
| 32 | 13068 | 22125 | 38105 | 66367 |
| 33 | 14156 | 24448 | 42981 | 76437 |
| 34 | 15325 | 27002 | 48466 | 88017 |
| 35 | 16582 | 29813 | 54637 | 101335 |
| 36 | 17933 | 32904 | 61579 | 116650 |
| 37 | 19386 | 36304 | 69389 | 134262 |
| 38 | 20947 | 40045 | 78175 | 154517 |
| 39 | 22626 | 44159 | 88059 | 177809 |
| 40 | 24430 | 48685 | 99179 | 204595 |

Table B opposite shows how $100 invested each year will accumulate at various rates of interest. For example, if a person invests $3,500 each year for 30 years and earns 12½% per annum, the total accumulation will be

$$\frac{\$3,500}{\$ \ 100} \times \$29,919 = \$1,047,165.$$

## HOW MUCH DO I NEED FOR RETIREMENT?

It is impossible to estimate generally how much any particular individual might need for his or her retirement years. To a great extent this will obviously depend upon the lifestyle you have had prior to retirement, the lifestyle you want after retirement, the state of your health, and scores of other factors. You should bear in mind that many of your present costs will disappear. For example, it is likely that your house will be paid for and that expenses associated with supporting your children will be over. Costs associated with your job (getting to work, business meals, entertaining, and so forth) will disappear.

On the other hand, if you are planning to do a lot of travelling or to take up an expensive hobby, you may have some new and very heavy costs.

Part of the overall problem in planning is that most people cannot make any realistic estimate of costs until they are quite close to retirement age. If you had asked a young person starting his career forty years ago what he might need for retirement, there is no way in the world he could have anticipated the effect of inflation. While in 1945, he might logically have thought that $5,000 a year would be an excellent retirement income, today such a sum would put him below the poverty level.

The best approach to take, therefore, is simply to put away as much as you possibly can towards retirement, bearing in mind that one seldom meets a retired person who complains that he or she has too much income.

However, before you can decide how much you can presently afford to save towards retirement, you will need to examine your present living costs. Although most people have a general idea of how much it costs them to live, they often do not know *how* they spend their money. Knowing the cost of important items such as food, clothing, shelter, transportation, etc., will give you some idea of possible ways to reduce some expenses in order to save towards retirement. It also gives you an idea of ways you are likely to spend your income after retirement.

## WHERE YOUR MONEY GOES

By keeping a daily record for one month, you can get a good idea of the amounts you are spending for different categories in your budget. Keep a small notebook on your person and jot down the amount of each purchase, no matter how small it may be. Whether it's a cup of coffee, a subway token, a stamp or a tube of toothpaste, write it down.

At the end of the month, add up the daily expenditures and list the amounts under the following headings:

Income tax
Utilities
House (mortgage, taxes, etc.)
Food
Clothing
Appliances
Furniture
Personal care
Medical and health
Cigarettes and alcohol
Life insurance
Automobile
Other transportation
Recreation
Personal spending (miscellaneous)
Gifts and donations
Vacation
Total

If you can keep this kind of record for several months, you will, of course, have an even better idea of how you spend your income and ways you can reduce some expenditures for retirement savings. As you get closer to retirement you will be able to make a better estimate of what you will need for the future and how some expenses will decrease.

## HOW MUCH DO I HAVE PUT AWAY?

Once again, estimating what your retirement income will be is essentially a function of how far away from retirement you are.

If you are 30, with several dependents, and working for a large company, it will be practically impossible for you to know how much of a pension you might ultimately get, how much will be payable under the government plans, and what assets you might accumulate over the next thirty or forty years.

Conversely, if you are just a year or so from retirement, you should be able to make a very respectable guess based on all these factors. If you are a member of a company pension plan, your personnel department should be able to give you a "ballpark estimate" of what your pension will be. Similarly, officials of the Department of Health and Welfare can probably give you the same sort of estimate with regard to Canada or Quebec Pension Plan payments and Old Age Security payments. You should also have a pretty good idea of what assets you have and how much income they generate. You might also take into account other assets. For example, you might be planning to sell that large house you own and move into an apartment. If so, you can get a feel for the value of the house. If it is worth, say, $150,000, it is likely that you could invest that money to produce $15,000 a year. (But don't forget that you may have to pay some of that in tax each year, and you'll have to pay rent on the apartment.)

And there is another factor to consider. Most people think only about the amount of income yielded by their investments. Suppose you have a portfolio of $250,000 which generates $25,000 a year. You *may* want to take into account the fact that you could sell off some of your portfolio annually to augment your income. Many people take the position that they will never touch their capital (usually because they are planning to leave it to their children) but you should recognize that your assets are available if you need to use them.

Now that we have looked at the general issues which are involved, let's turn to an examination of the specifics, starting with the retirement money which comes from the government.

## GOVERNMENT PLANS FOR RETIREMENT

There are two main government plans which give substantial support for retirement. These are the Old Age Security program (OAS) and the Canada Pension Plan (CPP). (Quebec has an analogous pension plan, the QPP, which is closely co-ordinated with the federal plan.) There are a number of other programs which are part of these plans, such as the Guaranteed Income Supplement (GIS) and the Spouse's Allowance, which are geared to the needs of those who have very low incomes. In addition, some provinces also have plans which give those who are 65 or over and in financial need, some extra funds. An example of this program is Ontario's "Guaranteed Annual Income System for Ontario Senior Citizens", known generally as GAINS.

In terms of impact, the most important of these plans is the OAS, which is available to most Canadian residents who are 65 or over.

## Old Age Security Payments

The Old Age Security Program is a plan under which most people who reach age 65 get a "pension" from the federal government. This plan is "universal" (subject to the comments below) in that the main criterion for receiving the payment is that you have reached age 65. No specific payment has been made to ensure eligibility nor is it necessary that you have been a member of the workforce. Indeed, for many women who have worked only in the home, the OAS payments are the first "income" they have ever received personally.

The payments themselves are taxable. If, for example, a wife receives only the OAS payments in the year, the effect of receiving the payments will be to reduce the marital deduction otherwise claimable by her husband. (Later in this chapter, we shall look at ways in which the tax bite can be reduced or deferred.)

The payments are adjusted to inflation each quarter. For example, at the start of 1983, the monthly payment was $251.12. At the start of 1984, it had risen to $263.78. And for the period January to March, 1985, the monthly payments rose to $273.80.

The importance of these payments as one "building block" of retirement funding is obvious. For 1985, most people aged 65 or over can count on at least $3,300 a year from this source alone which of course amounts to $6,600 for a couple living together.

While most people consider the OAS payments universal, this is not quite accurate. New rules were introduced in mid-1977 which put some limits on the amounts which could be received. A full pension will be paid to anyone who was age 25 or over and resident in Canada on July 1, 1977, or before that date and after they were 18 and:

**a)** were resident in Canada for a full ten years immediately prior to having the pension approved; or

**b)** were present in Canada after reaching age 18 and prior to the ten-year period referred to above, for a period equal to three times the length of absences in the ten-year period and, in addition, were resident for at least one year immediately prior to the approval of the application.

The idea behind the rule is to give a full pension only to those with longstanding ties to Canada. Those most likely to be "hurt" by the rules are relatively recent immigrants and those who plan to move abroad prior to the time they are eligible for a pension. If you don't meet the test for a full pension, you may be eligible for a reduced pension which is computed on the basis of the number of years you were resident in Canada after you reached 18, providing you have been in Canada for at least ten years.

If you lived in a country with which Canada has a social-security agreement, your years of residence in that country may count as years in Canada for the purpose of computing OAS eligibility. At the present time, Canada has such treaties with Belgium, France, Greece, Italy, Jamaica, Portugal, and the United States.

It is important to note that although you may automatically be entitled to OAS payments, you must apply for them. Application forms are available at any post office. The application should be sent to the federal department of Health and Welfare about six months before you reach age 65 (see Appendix B for the address).

## Guaranteed Income Supplement

There are two other aspects to the OAS program which are linked to need. The first is the Guaranteed Income Supplement (GIS) which is payable to either individuals or couples who have reached age 65 and who have little income aside from OAS. A very large number of Canadians who are 65 or over get either the full or partial GIS payments depending on the income of the recipient in the year prior to the payments. These payments, in the first quarter of 1985, are to a maximum of $325.41 for a single person and $211.93 for each of a married couple. Reduced payments are made when the recipient has exceeded a base rate (which varies from year to year). To get GIS payments, an application must be made annually to the federal department of Health and Welfare. Data of your income must be provided annually as well.

## Spouse's Allowance

A program similar to GIS, known as the Spouse's Allowance, is also run under the overall OAS program. This program is designed to give money to a person between the ages of 60 and 65 if his or her spouse is getting OAS and GIS. In essence, this program fills in the gap for low-income couples when one of them is too young to qualify for OAS and GIS. A similar program applicable to widows and widowers between the ages of 60 and 65 has been proposed and is expected to be effective in 1985. Once again, application must be made to Health and Welfare, Canada, which can provide details required both as to the magnitude of the benefits available and the data required.

## Supplemental Programs

You should also, if you have an extremely low income, check with your provincial social security agency to see whether you may be eligible for benefits under a provincial scheme. In Ontario, the GAINS program automatically makes payments to those residents of the province who receive federal GIS payments, and no separate application should be made.

The idea behind these various programs is to ensure that no senior citizen in Canada is in dire need. But the introduction in 1965 of the Canada Pension Plan should go a long way to eliminating the need for such supplemental programs. Obviously, one of the key elements of financial planning for retirement is to ensure that *you* are not one of the people who needs to apply for supplemental payments. At the same time, it is important to recognize that such plans exist as you may well find that there are people you know, perhaps parents or elderly relatives, who might be eligible for supplementary aid but who do not get it simply because they are unaware of its availability.

## The Canada (or Quebec) Pension Plan (CPP/QPP)

The second major federal program geared to retirement is the Canada (or Quebec) Pension Plan. This is an earnings-related pension plan in that the payments under it are linked to the years you have worked and the amounts you have contributed. Since January 1966, virtually everybody who is an employee or carries on business as a self-employed person has had to contribute to the Canada or Quebec Pension Plan which offers essentially the same benefits as the Canada Plan. Both the employer and the employee contribute 1.8 per cent of salary to the plan, though there is both a base below which one does not contribute and a maximum. In 1985, the base figure was $2,300 and the maximum was $23,400, although each of these figures will rise annually in the future. Thus, the top contribution for 1985 by each of the employer and employee (for people earning $23,400 a year or more) was 1.8 per cent of $21,100 or $379.80. If you are self-employed, you pay both contributions, for a total of $759.60. The annual contribution is deductible in computing your income for tax purposes.

Starting in the year you reach 65, a pension is paid even if you still continue to work. But if you do work, you will cease making contributions and will get no increased pension.

The pension is set according to a formula based on the amount of your contributions and the years during which you contributed to the plan. A person who retired in 1985 and had made maximum contributions would receive a basic pension of $435.42 a month, and this pension is indexed to take inflation into account. Credits are fully transferable between the Canada and Quebec plans, so that moving from Quebec to another province or vice-versa does not penalize you.

## Benefits Under the Canada and Quebec Pension Plans

What a lot of people are unaware of is that there is a whole range of benefits payable under these plans in addition to the pension. For example, if you are disabled for an extended period of time, there is a disability pension. A disabled person with a child under age 18 (or under age 25 if the child is attending school) will also get a payment in respect of each such child.

If you die leaving a spouse, the spouse will be entitled to a pension, as will an orphan under the ages of 18 or 25 if the child is at school. And there is also a death benefit which is payable to your estate when you die.

Benefits arising under the Canada or Quebec Pension Plans are fully taxable. It should be pointed out that they do not qualify for the "pension income deduction" under the Income Tax Act, which is discussed later when we deal with the tax rules associated with retirement.

It should be noted that the availability of the CPP/QPP makes it attractive for both spouses to be members. If you have an opportunity to employ your spouse or if your spouse gets a job and contributes, the spouse will also be eligible for CPP payments in due course.

In considering your potential retirement income, therefore, it is important to note that a fairly substantial amount may be coming from government sources. If both you and your spouse have reached age 65 and you contributed at the top rate to the CPP/QPP from the inception of the plans on January 1, 1966, the two of you, in 1985, would have received from OAS and CPP an annual income of about $12,000 a year. Perhaps this amount is not enough for you to live in the manner you would like, but it is certainly a decent starting base.

As we mentioned earlier, unless you are very close to retirement age, it is difficult to estimate just what your income will be from these sources. However, you can get information at any time about where you stand in terms of contributions made under the plans, by contacting the federal department of Health and Welfare.

Reproduced opposite is a chart showing the first quarter payments for 1985 under the CPP/QPP as well as the Old Age Security program. Note that most of these figures will increase in the future because of the program of indexing.

## PRIVATE PENSION PLANS

In addition to pensions funded or sponsored by the government, a very large number of Canadians also provide for retirement through private plans. These may be divided into two main groupings: employer-sponsored plans and self-funded plans. We shall examine each separately.

### Employer Plans

Most, if not all of the larger companies in Canada, along with most public and quasi-public institutions, have registered pension plans for their employees. Usually, both the employee and employer contribute to these plans, which are not subject to tax. When an employee reaches retirement age, a pension will be payable.

But there are almost as many variations on the plans as there are plans. The plans may differ as to:

## GOVERNMENT BENEFITS – 1985

| Canada/Quebec Pension Plan | CPP | QPP |
|---|---|---|
| Maximum Monthly Retirement Pension | $ 435.42 | $ 435.42 |
| Death Benefits | | |
| (i) Lump Sum | 2,340.00 | 2,340.00 |
| (ii) Maximum Monthly Spouse's Pension | | |
| under age 55 | 250.84 | 387.68 |
| 55 – 65 | 250.84 | 450.38 |
| over age 65 | 261.25 | 261.25 |
| (iii) Monthly Orphan's Pension | 87.56 | 29.00 |
| Disability Benefits | | |
| (i) Maximum Monthly Contributor's Pension | 414.13 | 550.97 |
| (ii) Monthly Child Benefit | 87.56 | 29.00 |
| Maximum Annual Contributions | | |
| (i) Self-employed | 759.60 | 759.60 |
| (ii) Employer or Employee | 379.80 | 379.80 |

*Old Age Security (OAS)*     *Maximum Monthly Benefit Level (January – March 1985)*

| | |
|---|---|
| Basic Benefit | $ 273.80 |
| Guaranteed Income Supplement (GIS) | $ 325.41 (single)<br>423.86 (couple) |
| Spouses's Allowance: | |
| (i) paid to people between ages 60 and 65 whose spouse receives both OAS and GIS | 485.73 |
| (ii) paid to single recipients who are surviving spouses of deceased pensioners | 536.26 |

**a)** the percentage of income contributed annually by both employer and employee;

**b)** retirement age;

**c)** indexing of benefits;

**d)** payments to spouses when the employee dies;

    **e)** other benefits associated with the plans such as disability payments, death benefits, insurance, and so forth;

    **f)** vesting, that is, the time at which you are guaranteed a pension from the plan. (If you are not "vested" and you leave the plan, you may only be entitled to your own contributions back.);

    **g)** the ability to increase your pension by making additional contributions, usually in respect of years spent working during which you were not a plan member; and

    **h)** portability, which refers to the ability to take your "credits" from one plan and shift them to another plan with another employer and still get full pension coverage.

## The Money Purchase Plan

There are two basic types of plan which are offered. One is known as the "money purchase" plan. In this type of plan, your contributions and those of your employer are kept and invested on your behalf. When it comes time to retire, the money standing to your account is used to purchase a pension. The size of your pension, therefore, depends to a great degree on the success of the plan administrators in investing the funds.

## The Defined Benefit Plan

The second type of plan is known as the "defined benefit plan". Under this plan, your pension is linked to a formula based on your years of service and, typically, your average income over the last three or five years of work. For example, if the plan calls for a 2 per cent per year pension based on your last three years' average salary and you worked for the company for 30 years, your pension, if the average of your income for the last three years of service was $30,000, would be computed as follows: 30 years of service times 2 per cent = 60 per cent, times $30,000 = $18,000.

    This sort of plan puts the onus on the employer to contribute enough money to meet the obligations of the plan if its investments do not achieve the goal. This often happens in periods of high inflation during which employee salaries have risen swiftly and the final years' earnings are much higher than might otherwise have been anticipated.

# Investigate Your Pension Plan

Experience has shown that most employees are almost totally unaware of the workings of their pension plans and the benefits which they may be entitled to. However, administrators of the plans (who can usually be contacted through the personnel office) have an obligation to inform employees about the plans. In many provinces there are regulations governing the information that must be disclosed to the participants annually or triennually and include details about benefits payable on death, termination of employment, disability and many other points. This information is normally contained in an "Employee Benefit Statement" which should be carefully reviewed when received. It is important *at any stage of your career* to understand how the pension plan you are in operates, for only after you understand this can you make the appropriate moves in terms of long-range financial planning. Once again, it is obvious that as you come closer to retirement, you should be able to make a better estimate as to what your pension entitlement should be.

But we should stress that it is almost equally important to find out what your spouse would get if you die either before or after retirement. And if you have a situation that is out of the ordinary — say you are living "common law" or have young children dependent upon you — you should also check to see whether any coverage or benefits will apply to them.

Generally speaking, contributions which you make each year to such a plan are deductible in computing your income for tax purposes, so long as the annual payment does not exceed $3,500. Employer contributions are also deductible by the employer. The pensions are fully taxable when received.

Some employers offer plans known as "deferred profit-sharing plans" or "employee profit-sharing plans", either in addition to pension plans or instead of such plans. These plans vary substantially from company to company, and if you are a member of such a plan, it is worthwhile getting further information about it from your personnel office.

A word is also in order about small companies. Revenue Canada has, over the years, imposed stringent limits on the ability of small companies to have pension plans where, as is usually the case, major shareholders who are also employees get a large percentage of the benefits. If you are a major shareholder to such a company, you may want to look into setting up a pension plan, and professional advice should be sought from an insurance company, trust company or benefit consultant.

Very often, shareholder/employees, like others who are not covered by pension plans, fund their own retirement through the use of Registered Retirement Savings Plans (RRSPs) which are discussed below under the heading of "self-funded plans".

## SELF-FUNDED PLANS: RRSPs

As far back as 1957, the government recognized that people who were not able to be in an employer pension plan would be at a distinct disadvantage in saving for retirement. It therefore introduced a tax-based concept to allow for private retirement savings, known as an RRSP. These plans have the general characteristics of a money-purchase pension plan, but as with pension plans, there is a huge variety of options which are available. The key, however, is to understand the tax benefits.

A person who sets up such a plan (known as the "annuitant") does so with a bank, trust company, insurance company, brokerage house, or with some other agency which offers the services. The individual makes a contribution annually (if possible) to the plan and the funds are invested. The income generated within the plan is free of tax. Eventually, the funds will be withdrawn in some form and will be taxed at that time.

At the present time, the maximum amount which an individual can contribute and deduct annually depends upon whether he or she is covered by a pension plan in the year. If he or she is a member of a plan (and this essentially means that he or she would be entitled to a benefit under the plan in respect of that year at some point) the maximum deductible contribution is the lesser of 20 per cent of earned income (basically, wages, salary, income from self-employment, net rentals, alimony, or maintenance received) and $3,500, less any contribution made to a pension plan in the year. If he or she is not covered by a pension plan, the deductible amount is the lesser of 20 per cent of earned income or $5,500.

In the Budget of February 1984, it was proposed that the RRSP contribution limits be substantially increased, with the applicable percentage of income dropped from 20 per cent to 18 per cent. Under the proposal, the contribution limit would be $10,000 for 1985, but at time of writing this proposal has not yet been enacted. As of 1984, a new proposal allows full-time farmers who dispose of their farm property to transfer up to $120,000 of taxable capital gains to an RRSP on a tax-free basis. While most institutions offering the plans stress the benefit of getting the annual tax deduction, the most important benefit lies in allowing the money to grow on a tax-free basis for an extended period of time. As we pointed out at the start of this chapter, there are tremendous benefits to be had from putting money in this plan early and leaving it there for as long as possible. It is for this reason that the government has put strict limits on the amount of money which can be put in annually and why it imposes a penalty tax if you put too much in.

## Options Upon Termination of RRSPs

The RRSP plan must be terminated by the end of the year in which you turn age 71. At this time you have four options. First, you might just pull the money out of the plan; in this case you would pay tax on the full amount. Second, you can arrange to buy a life annuity from an insurance company which will make payments to you so long as you live. If you choose this option, you can arrange for the annuity to be guaranteed for a period of years (say 10 or 15) so that if you die, the money will go to your heirs. Or you can buy a joint annuity which will be payable so long as either you or your spouse lives.

A third option allows you to transfer the funds to a Registered Retirement Income Fund (RRIF). Under this scheme, you get payments which increase annually from the date you make the transfer until you reach age 90.

Finally, you may purchase an annuity which will make payments to you until you reach 90 years of age. If your spouse is younger than you, and you so choose, the payments can be made until he or she reaches the age of 90.

When it comes time to do something with your plan, you should seek advice from one of the many experts in this area as to which is the best idea for you. You might get one of the many books published annually about RRSPs, talk to somebody at the institution which carries your plan, speak to your lawyer or accountant or to an insurance agent who specializes in annuities. There are now annuity brokers who go out and shop on the investors' behalf for the best annuity quote.

There are provisions in the Income Tax Act which allow the tax-free transfer of your RRSP to your spouse if you die before the plan has been wound up.

## A COMPARISON OF ANNUITIES AT DIFFERENT INTEREST RATES
### Monthly Incomes per $10,000 commencing age 65

| Year | Male No guarantee | Female No guarantee | Male 15 year guarantee Indexed at 4% | Joint & Last Survivor No guarantee | Joint & Last Survivor 15 year guarantee Indexed at 4% | Term Certain to Age 90 | RRIF |
|---|---|---|---|---|---|---|---|
| | | | | **Interest Rate: 10%** | | | |
| 1 | 103.60 | 93.63 | 67.84 | 86.30 | 60.48 | 84.32 | 36.04 |
| 3 | 103.60 | 93.63 | 73.38 | 86.30 | 64.42 | 84.32 | 43.70 |
| 5 | 103.60 | 93.63 | 79.36 | 86.30 | 70.75 | 84.32 | 52.96 |
| 10 | 103.60 | 93.63 | 96.56 | 86.30 | 86.08 | 84.32 | 85.54 |
| 15 | 103.60 | 93.63 | 117.48 | 86.30 | 104.73 | 84.32 | 138.02 |
| 20 | 103.60 | 93.63 | 142.93 | 86.30 | 127.42 | 84.32 | 222.54 |
| 25 | 103.60 | 93.63 | 173.89 | 86.30 | 155.03 | 84.32 | 326.02 |
| | | | | **Interest Rate: 12½%** | | | |
| 1 | 119.29 | 109.19 | 80.89 | 101.59 | 74.07 | 99.95 | 36.79 |
| 3 | 119.29 | 109.19 | 87.49 | 101.59 | 80.11 | 99.95 | 46.68 |
| 5 | 119.29 | 109.19 | 94.63 | 101.59 | 86.65 | 99.95 | 59.19 |
| 10 | 119.29 | 109.19 | 115.13 | 101.59 | 105.42 | 99.95 | 106.99 |
| 15 | 119.29 | 109.19 | 140.08 | 101.59 | 128.27 | 99.95 | 193.14 |
| 20 | 119.29 | 109.19 | 170.42 | 101.59 | 156.05 | 99.95 | 348.38 |
| 25 | 119.29 | 109.19 | 207.35 | 101.59 | 189.86 | 99.95 | 528.29 |
| | | | | **Interest Rate: 15%** | | | |
| 1 | 135.02 | 124.84 | 94.43 | 117.18 | 88.30 | 115.95 | 37.55 |
| 3 | 135.02 | 124.84 | 102.14 | 117.18 | 95.51 | 115.95 | 49.79 |
| 5 | 135.02 | 124.84 | 110.47 | 117.18 | 103.30 | 115.95 | 65.98 |
| 10 | 135.02 | 124.84 | 134.40 | 117.18 | 125.68 | 115.95 | 133.14 |
| 15 | 135.02 | 124.84 | 163.52 | 117.18 | 152.91 | 115.95 | 268.22 |
| 20 | 135.02 | 124.84 | 198.95 | 117.18 | 186.03 | 115.95 | 539.90 |
| 25 | 135.02 | 124.84 | 242.05 | 117.18 | 226.34 | 115.95 | 944.60 |

The above information was supplied by the Standard Life Assurance Company.

# Selecting an RRSP Plan

Selecting a plan is not the easiest of chores, as there are literally hundreds to choose from, and you will have to make some decisions. For example, many plans are conservative and invest only in guaranteed-income certificates of a trust company or bank. Some invest in common stock; others go into mutual funds or invest in fairly risky oil and gas ventures. Still others invest in mortgages. It is also possible to set up a self-administered plan, one where you make the investment decisions, although this is the most costly of the options in terms of fees and charges and should only be chosen by relatively sophisticated investors.

You should also be aware that the government imposes limitations as to what investments a plan can hold, and while the list is large, it precludes investing in private companies, most mortgages on a home owned by you or a relative, or gold bullion.

While some sophisticated taxpayers use RRSPs as a form of income averaging, collapsing the plan to get the use of the money, for the vast majority of people the funds in the plan should remain inviolate. If you withdraw funds which represent retirement savings from earlier years, these savings can never be replaced, since you cannot make a contribution for a past year in which you did not pay or in respect of which you withdrew your funds.

A few other items should be noted.

First, if you have to borrow money to fund your RRSP, you cannot deduct the interest charges in computing income. But, in many cases, it may still be to your advantage to borrow rather than lose a year of contributions.

Second, you may contribute to the plan for a particular tax year up to 60 days after the end of the year. For most years, this means a contribution as late as March 1 will give you a tax deduction for the previous year. However, because the benefits which come from earning money in the plan are tax free, it is better, if you have the funds, to make your contribution as early in the tax year as you can.

Finally, the income which you get from the plan, either through an annuity or an RRIF, qualifies for the annual pension-income deduction of up to $1,000, providing you are age 65 or over. We shall examine this deduction in more detail later in this chapter.

You should also be aware that there are two other tax-planning ideas which can be implemented using RRSPs. The first is known as the "spousal plan". The second involves using a technique known as a "roll-over".

## The Spousal Plan

Since 1974, the Income Tax Act has allowed a person who is eligible to put money into an RRSP to put that money into a plan where the annuitant is his or her spouse. It should be stressed that the amount of money which can be contributed annually is limited precisely to the amount the contributor could have put in his or her own plan. Further, this is an option, so that to the extent funds are put into a spousal plan in any year, that amount cannot be put into a contributor's plan. For example, if you had the right to put $5,500 into your own plan in 1984, you could put anything up to $5,500 into your spouse's plan, but you must reduce your own contribution accordingly.

There is an obvious social reason for making a spousal contribution. This allows a working spouse or higher-income spouse to provide a retirement-income fund for the other spouse. Usually, this will be done when the contributing spouse is satisfied that his or her retirement needs are well in hand.

But there are major tax benefits as well. First, in the usual case, the annuitant of the spousal plan has little or no income, whereas the contributing spouse does have income. The creation of a spousal plan, which will end up providing a pension to the "non-working" spouse, ensures that the pension income generated by that plan will be taxed at a lower rate than would have been the case if the contributed funds simply went to increase the pension of the "working" spouse.

Second, the pension generated will be eligible for the $1,000 pension-income deduction (discussed later) and should ensure that each of the two spouses, upon retirement, can get up to $1,000 of tax-free pension income.

Because some people used this plan to shift income from one spouse to another over a very short period of time, a rule was introduced that if the funds are withdrawn in a lump sum within a three-year period of the contribution having been made, the money will be taxed to the contributing spouse, not to the annuitant. This rule is waived where the contributing spouse has died, one or other of the parties has become a non-resident, or if there is a marital breakdown evidenced by a legal separation or divorce.

The plans are particularly attractive in situations where one spouse is the source of most of the family funds, has made substantial provision for retirement, and is satisfied that the marriage is secure. If any of these elements is missing, it might be better simply to contribute to your own plan.

## Roll-Overs

A second important use to which an RRSP can be put is to shelter certain types of income which would otherwise be taxable when received. These amounts can be transferred on a tax-free basis (known as a "roll-over") to an RRSP *in addition to* any annual contributions which you are eligible to make. The types of income which can be transferred are:

• a pension or superannuation payment, whether it is a periodic payment or a lump sum;

• a pension, supplement, or spouse's allowance under the Old Age Security Act;

• a payment under the Canada or Quebec Pension plans;

• a taxable amount from a deferred profit-sharing plan; and

• within limits, based upon years of service with the employer, a retiring allowance, which is sometimes known as a "golden handshake".

It should be noted, however, that these amounts must go to your own RRSP and cannot be transferred to that of your spouse.

The benefits of using the roll-over can be seen through a couple of examples.

Suppose that you were forced to retire from a job and are getting a pension. However, you find that because you can do some consulting and have a flow of investment income, you do not need your full pension income to live on. If you take the pension anyway, you will pay tax on it. But you could, alternatively, transfer all or part of it to an RRSP. If you do this, you defer the tax which you would otherwise pay in the year you get the pension income and boost the capital of your RRSP, ensuring a larger annuity after you have passed age 71.

It is possible to arrange for the company paying your pension to transfer the funds directly to your RRSP, and if this is done, the company will withhold no tax and the money need never come into your hands until you "annuitize" your RRSP. Of course, if at any time you decide you need more of your pension money, you simply contact the payer and have the pension diverted back to you.

The roll-over is often used for people who continue working past the age of 65 and are fortunate enough not to need the money they are getting from the Canada Pension Plan payments or Old Age Security payments.

The roll-over can also be very attractive for a spouse who has never been in the workforce if he or she is being supported by the other spouse and the two of them do not need extra income. Suppose, for example, Mrs. Jones is a lawyer who at age 68 is still earning a substantial income. Mr. Jones turns 65 and finds himself getting well over $3,000 a year from OAS. The effect of getting this money will reduce the marital exemption Mrs. Jones can claim for Mr. Jones because his income is over the tax-free limit of (in 1985) $510. If Mr. Jones were to transfer all his OAS (except for $510) to an RRSP, the following would result:

First, Mr. Jones is creating his own retirement fund on a tax-sheltered basis. When he reaches age 72, he can have his own "pension" from his RRSP. Second, in getting this second pension, the family will have two $1,000 pension-income deductions instead of just one. Third, his income for tax purposes will be reduced to just $510, which means that Mrs. Jones will continue, from the time he is 65 until the year in which he turns 71, to get the full marital deduction for Mr. Jones. And finally, Mr. Jones is able, through his RRSP, to make tax-sheltered investments.

This option, obviously, is only available to families which have enough income to enable them to put away the "extra" into an RRSP, but, where this is the case, it is a highly recommended procedure.

While most people think in terms of using the roll-over only when they are older, it should be observed that there may well be situations where relatively young people can use the procedure.

For example, suppose you have been working for a particular company and decide to leave for a new job. You find that your pension with the first company is not vested, and the new company does not have a pension plan. You will be entitled to a refund of your contributions to the pension plan of the company you were working for. If you just take this money, you will pay tax on the full amount and end up with no pension savings for those particular working years. But you could, instead, roll-over the money you get to an RRSP, thus avoiding the immediate tax liability and, at the same time, retaining intact the capital which you have already saved towards retirement.

By the same token, you might find that you were laid off and given several thousands of dollars of "severance pay". Such a payment would qualify as a retiring allowance, and you would be able to put at least a portion of it into an RRSP. This might be an attractive option if you have other sources of income, say, because you got a new job shortly after having been laid-off the old one. Whenever you get income which fits into the qualifying categories, it is worthwhile to examine whether a roll-over is appropriate in your situation.

## SPECIAL TAX RULES FOR OLDER CANADIANS

Over the years, a number of special rules have been introduced into the Income Tax Act which are of particular interest to older Canadians.

In particular, you should be aware that anybody who has reached age 65 is entitled to a special deduction. In 1985, this deduction amounted to $2,590, and it will increase over time as the tax system is indexed to inflation.

And there is the pension-income deduction to which we have already alluded. This falls into two categories. If you are age 65 or older, you can deduct the lesser of $1,000 or your "pension income" for the year. Pension income includes a life annuity out of a pension plan (other than an OAS or CPP/QPP payment), an annuity out of an RRSP, a payment from a RRIF, an annuity from a deferred profit-sharing plan, or the income element of an annuity which does not come out of one of the tax-sheltered funds. While OAS and CPP/QPP payments do not qualify, foreign-source pensions, such as a payment from the U.S. Social Security Plan, would qualify.

You can see by these rules why the roll-over of OAS payments to an RRSP will be attractive as we showed earlier in the example of Mr. Jones. The OAS payment itself is not eligible for the pension-income deduction, but the annuity from his RRSP, which was funded with the OAS payments, is eligible.

If you are under age 65, you will also qualify for the pension-income deduction, but with some limitations. First, a payment from an RRSP will not qualify until you reach age 65. This is done to ensure that people do not annuitize RRSPs at too early an age to generate the pension-income deduction. Second, unless you are disabled, if you use the roll-over provisions prior to age 60, you cannot claim the pension-income deduction.

It is interesting to note how much income a married couple

could shelter through the use of just the basic deductions when they are both 65.

Using 1985 deductions and exemptions, we get the following:

| | |
|---|---|
| Personal deduction | $4,140 |
| Age deduction | 2,590 |
| Federal tax credit | 1,432.50* |
| Total | $8,162.50 |

\* Each taxpayer is allowed a $100 tax credit which starts to be reduced when federal tax exceeds $6,000. The figure of $1,432.50 is the $100 credit converted to its equivalent as a deduction.

In addition, the couple may each be entitled to a $1,000 pension-income deduction and perhaps each might claim a $1,000 investment-income deduction (which is discussed later in this chapter). In addition, the couple may also have available to them other deductions for charitable donations, medical expenses, RRSP contributions, and so forth.

But to get the maximum benefit, each of the spouses must have one or more sources of independent income. This is why, if financial circumstances allow, tax planning should be geared to ensuring that each partner in a married couple has pension income and investment income.

In some cases, a spouse may have eligibility for certain deductions, most notably the age deduction and the pension-and investment-income deductions, but be unable to use them. For example, if one spouse had $1,000 of investment income and $1,000 of pension income and no other income (say, because OAS payments were rolled-over to an RRSP), that spouse would be eligible for $2,000 worth of deductions in respect of these sources of income as well as the age deduction. But since there is no tax liability, and indeed because this spouse is dependent upon the other spouse, the deductions appear to be "wasted". For this reason, it is possible to transfer deductions from a supported to a supporting spouse. This is done through filling in the appropriate schedule which comes with the Income Tax Return (in past years, this has been Schedule 3) and sending it in with the return of the supporting spouse. Whenever one spouse is claiming the other as a dependent, the supporting spouse should fill in Schedule 3 to see whether there are some deductions which can be transferred, thus avoiding the "waste".

# OTHER INVESTMENTS AS A SOURCE OF RETIREMENT FUNDING

If at all possible, an overall plan to provide for your retirement should include investing. It should be pointed out that being a member of a pension plan or having an RRSP constitutes a form of investment. Indeed, because you get a deduction for the "capital" you invest and because the income generated is free of tax, fully using your capacity to save through such plans is crucial. But as we noted earlier, it is for this very reason that the government has put strict limits on the annual amount you can save under these deferred plans.

A second very important investment is the family home. There are two tax-oriented reasons for this. First, the "income" produced is tax free. In the case of a family home, the "income" from the investment is rent-free accommodation. Second, when the house is sold, it usually will produce a capital gain which is free of tax. This is known as the "principal residence exemption". (You may lose a part of this tax-free treatment if at any time you rent out your house. If you are planning to rent your house, you should consult a lawyer about steps which might be taken to ensure the best tax results.)

Your house should be considered a retirement investment for a couple of reasons. First, normally, by the time you retire, you will own it outright, reducing your accommodation costs significantly. (You should also check to see whether your province is one of those which gives seniors a tax break in connection with property taxes. Often this break is given through reduced provincial income taxes which you might otherwise pay.) Second, because most houses have escalated in value significantly in recent years, you may find that your house is worth a significant amount of money. If, like many older people, you decide to give up a large house in order to move to smaller accommodations, you should remember that when you sell the house, you will be able to get the full value free of tax which will produce additional capital for investment.

Because the house is such a valuable investment, most advisers will tell you that you should eliminate or reduce your mortgage as quickly as possible. Suppose that you have just had a $10,000 windfall. If you invest the money at 10 per cent to earn an extra $1,000, after taxes are paid on the interest, you might just net $600 or $700. But if you have an outstanding mortgage at, say, 12 per cent, reducing the mortgage will save you $1,238.28 a year on your payments, perhaps, in effect, doubling your return on the investment.

Of course, there are a wide range of potential investments which you might be interested in. Many people collect things such as coins, stamps, antiques, or paintings. This kind of collecting may well be viewed as investment, not just as a hobby. The major problem with these forms of investments is that when you reach retirement, you may not wish to dispose of them for the purpose of adding to your capital. Indeed, one of the joys of retirement may be to spend more time with these hobbies. Thus, while collecting may be viewed as a form of investment, it seldom is a practical method of providing for retirement, though the option certainly exists.

Usually, when you are considering investments, you will be thinking in terms of stocks, bonds, real estate, and the like. A good basic type of investment, for example, is the acquisition of Canada Savings Bonds which are very safe, can be turned into cash at any time, and provide a fair return. In addition, if your employer offers a payroll deduction plan, you can acquire bonds quite painlessly. These plans are geared so that after one year, the bond is fully paid for.

Of course, the stock market attracts a lot of potential investors. It should be pointed out that in this area, you have to make a number of crucial decisions. For example, are you interested in getting a flow of income through dividends or are you more interested in the potential increase in the value of the shares? The decision may dictate whether you invest in common shares (more risk) or preferred shares (less risk and virtually guaranteed annual income). If you are going to invest in the stock market, you should shop around for a broker who is willing to advise you, but you should be prepared to tell the broker exactly what your goals are.

More conservative investors may want to buy guaranteed-income certificates from trust companies or banks or other forms of debt where one is assured of getting an income flow, though usually there will be no possibility of getting a capital gain.

Real estate is also a very attractive form of investment, but you should be wary of this type of acquisition unless you know something about the subject or can invest with somebody else who is an expert. While there are great profits to be made through real-estate investments, a surprisingly large number of people who make these investments do, in fact, lose money.

# TAX RULES ABOUT INVESTING

You should be aware that there are a large number of tax rules which apply to various investments and the crucial thing is to ensure that you get the best *after tax* return.

The most important of these rules is that up to the first $1,000 of Canadian source investment income is free of tax. This applies to Canadian dividends, capital gains from selling Canadian securities or interest from Canadian sources. The effect of this rule is that if you are a modest investor, you may well find that all your investment income can be received on a tax-free basis.

The second tax rule you should be familiar with relates to dividends from Canadian sources. When you get a dividend, it must be reported for tax purposes as 1.5 times the amount you receive. But you then get a credit equal to one-half the dividend. In many cases, this will wipe out your tax liability in respect of the dividends and may actually go to reduce your other taxes.

**Example 1:** Suppose your taxable income in 1985 was $15,000 and you live in Ontario. You will pay tax on each additional dollar at a rate of about 30 per cent. Suppose that you got $100 in dividends and have already used your $1,000 investment-income deduction. Your tax calculation will be as follows:

| | |
|---|---|
| Cash dividend | $100 |
| Dividend reported | 150 |
| Tax (30 per cent) | 45 |
| Tax credit | 50 |
| Tax liability | ($ 5) |

In this case, not only do you not pay any tax on the dividend, but your taxes in respect of other income will be reduced by $5.

**Example 2:** The facts are the same as above, but you had no other investment income. You would calculate your tax burden in the same way as above, but you will eligible to deduct $150 (the dividend reported for tax purposes) from taxable income. Under the investment-income deduction, you can claim the lesser of your dividends (as reported for tax purposes) and $1,000.

**Example 3:** The facts are the same as above, but your taxable income was in excess of $62,000. This means that in Ontario, the next dollar of income is taxable at about 51.1 per cent. Again, we shall assume that you have already used your $1,000 investment-income deduction.

| Cash dividend | $100 |
|---|---|
| Dividend reported | 150 |
| Tax (51.1 per cent) | 76.65 |
| Dividend tax credit | 50 |
| Tax liability | $ 26.65 |

This represents the highest tax which will be paid in Ontario on a $100 dividend. The figure will differ from province to province depending upon provincial tax rates, with the lowest tax being paid in Alberta and the highest in Newfoundland and Quebec.

We should point out that these examples have been simplified. The actual calculation as done on a tax return is very different, but the result is as we have shown here.

If you get a capital gain, you report only one-half the gain for tax purposes. The effect of this is to apply tax at just one-half your normal rate.

Interest is fully taxable with no associated special tax rules, except for being eligible for the $1,000 investment-income deduction.

A number of rules of thumb can be given.

**1.** If your combined federal-provincial tax rate is 33⅓ per cent or below (under about $18,000 in taxable income in 1985), all dividends will be tax free in your hands, and some of the excess credit will reduce other tax liability.

**2.** The rate of tax for very high income taxpayers on dividends will be between 25 per cent and 27 per cent maximum.

**3.** The tax on capital gains is higher for all taxpayers than the rate on dividends until you get to a taxable-income range of about $62,000. At this level, the tax on dividends and capital gains is about the same.

**4.** If you are trying to make a choice between investments producing interest and those producing dividends, the basic rule of thumb is that you must get 1.5 times the yield as interest to get the same after-tax return on dividends. That is, an 8 per cent dividend is worth 12 per cent in interest. If you can get 13 per cent in interest, take it. If you can only get 11 per cent in interest, opt for the dividends.

## THE QUEBEC STOCK SAVINGS PLAN

Residents of Quebec have a special savings vehicle available to them which should be looked at by anybody in that province who is getting involved in a program of financial planning through investing.

The Quebec Stock Savings Plan (QSSP) allows very attractive deductions for taxpayers who buy newly issued shares of Quebec-based corporations. It should be stressed that the deduction will apply only to your Quebec provincial taxes, and will not reduce your federal tax liability.

The following categories of stock qualify for the deduction:

• Common shares with full voting rights issued by eligible corporations, which are not redeemable at the corporation's request, and which are issued through a public share issue on the primary market.

• Subordinate voting shares of eligible corporations which meet the conditions set out above.

• Preferred shares which meet the conditions set out above, issued by developing corporations and convertible at any time into common shares with full voting rights.

• Preferred shares which meet the conditions set out above, issued by developing corporations and convertible at any time into subordinate voting shares.

The amount you may deduct in respect of any particular purchase will vary depending upon the nature of the investment. The following list shows the percentage of the cost you can deduct in respect of various categories:

• Common shares with full voting rights issued by a developing corporation: 150 per cent of the cost of the shares.

• Preferred shares issued by a developing corporation and convertible into common shares with full voting rights: 150 per cent of the cost of the shares.

• Subordinate voting shares issued by a developing corporation: 100 per cent of the cost of the shares.

• Preferred shares issued by a developing corporation and convertible into subordinate voting shares: 100 per cent of the cost of the shares.

- Common shares with full voting rights issued by a corporation, the assets of which are less than $1 billion and which is not a developing corporation: 100 per cent of the cost of the shares.

- Subordinate voting shares issued by a corporation, the assets of which are less than $1 billion and which is not a developing corporation: in 1984, 100 per cent of the cost of the shares; after 1984, 75 per cent.

- Common shares with full voting rights and subordinate voting shares issued by a corporation, the assets of which are equal to or more than $1 billion: in 1984, 75 per cent of the cost of the shares; after 1984, 50 per cent.

The maximum amount you can deduct in any given year is the lesser of 20 per cent of your income or $20,000 minus:

**a)** contributions to a registered pension plan or an RRSP; and

**b)** 150 per cent of the cost of the shares of the Fonds de solidarité des travailleurs du Québec for which a deduction is claimed in the tax year.

Unlike the definition of earned income for RRSP purposes, the term "income" for the QSSP includes investment income and capital gains.

The plan is opened by setting up a special QSSP account with a stock broker, bank, trust company, savings or credit union or other financial institution. The institution which deals with the account takes care of the tax documentation which must be attached to your provincial tax return.

The major attraction of this plan is that not only do you get a deduction for your purchases, but if the shares are held for at least two years, any gain at the end of the period will be free of Quebec taxes. Of course, in terms of your federal tax return, you will get no deduction for the purchases, and gains or losses on the holdings in the QSSP are treated as though you owned them personally. Any dividends received are reported, both for provincial and federal purposes, as though the investor received them directly.

There are a number of aspects which must be considered before investing through a QSSP. It is clear, for example, that if you do not contribute to a pension plan or an RRSP, you increase your ability to use the QSSP. But you should remember that a pension or RRSP contribution will result in deductions from both federal and provincial taxes while a QSSP deduction applies only to provincial taxes.

On the other hand, the "payout" from a pension plan or RRSP is ultimately fully taxable both federally and provincially while the QSSP payout is tax free if you meet the minimum holding requirements.

If you have to borrow money to fund a QSSP investment, the interest is deductible for both federal and provincial tax purposes. But if you borrow for your RRSP or pension contribution, the interest is non-deductible.

You should also remember that while you can deduct contributions made to a spousal RRSP, there is no such thing as a spousal QSSP.

The QSSP is an extremely important tax savings device, but should only be used after discussing your overall tax strategy with an expert. There are some excellent brochures available which deal with the QSSP, giving examples of possible tax savings and strategies. One of the best we have seen is put out by the Montreal Stock Exchange and should be available from all stock brokers in the province of Quebec.

## GET ADVICE

We cannot over-emphasize that any successful investment program, other than simply buying Canada Savings Bonds or putting your money in term deposits or Guaranteed Income Certificates, requires expert advice. There are many reputable investment dealers (see your phone book if you have nobody who can recommend one) who will be more than happy to help you with an investment plan. Usually these experts get paid a commission based upon what you buy and sell, although, if you have a very large amount to invest, you may get very personalized portfolio-management advice for which you pay a fee.

The second important point is to recognize that in the space available, we cannot canvass all types of investments or go into all the ramifications and permutations related to the tax aspects. Most investment dealers and almost all large accounting firms publish pamphlets which deal with the tax aspects of investing. There is no charge for these pamphlets and brochures, and they often give very valuable detail about investing and the tax system.

We might also point out that many courses are given to help

the neophyte understand various types of investments. You might check out community colleges and night courses offered by your local school system for such courses.

And finally, there are a wide range of books available in your library or in the "business" section of bookstores which deal in great detail with aspects of investing (see "Further Reading").

Investing to produce retirement funding should not be ignored simply because you know nothing about it. There is probably no other area in which so much expert advice is available as there is for those who want to learn how to make their money grow.

## LIFE INSURANCE AS PART OF RETIREMENT PLANNING

In terms of any retirement planning, insurance should play a role, though that role may vary over a period of time.

Probably the most important single function which insurance serves is to guarantee that a fund of money will be available to support those who are dependent upon you in the event of your death before you have had a chance to accumulate sufficient assets.

For example, if you are a person, say, 35 years old, with a spouse and two dependent children, an assessment of your situation may show that your company pension is not yet vested, you have very little in your RRSP, and your savings are minimal because most of your income is going to meet current obligations. You should be carrying sufficient insurance to provide the money which your dependents will need if you were to die. A quick rule of thumb is to figure out their cash needs on an annual basis, allow something for inflation, and figure that the money can be invested at 10 per cent. Then, you work out how much you already have in assets. The difference between what you have and what would be needed should be filled in with insurance.

**Example:**

| | | | |
|---|---|---|---|
| Annual cash needs | $35,000 | Assets needed (yielding 10%) | $350,000 |
| | | Less existing assets | 30,000 |
| | | Insurance required | $320,000 |

Of course, as you acquire more assets yourself, the amount of insurance needed will likely drop.

The importance of life insurance is two-fold. First, it can provide a very substantial amount of capital at the time when it may be most needed — when the main income earner dies. Second, the money will be received by the beneficiary of the policy on a tax-free basis. This means that if you buy $250,000 of insurance, you know that if you die, your family will have the full amount at its disposal.

Insurance has a number of other roles aside and apart from creating an instant pool of money to protect your family. For example, when you are assessing your insurance needs, consider your debts. Insurance should be sufficient to meet all outstanding debts (including any mortgage on your home) so that in the event that you die prematurely, your family is not faced with the possible loss of the home, car, or other valuable assets for which you might have borrowed money.

Insurance is often put in place to ensure that funds are available to a business to help it continue to run if the key person were to die. And it is used to create a fund to pay off tax liabilities which may arise as a consequence of death. (Some of these uses of insurance will be discussed in the chapter dealing with "estate planning".)

You should be aware that in almost every situation, the premiums you pay for insurance will not be deductible in computing your income.

## Term Insurance

While there are literally scores of variations on insurance policies, there are only two basic types.

"Term insurance" is protection which offers "pure" insurance coverage. There is no saving or investment aspect. Typically, you buy this insurance and pay annually for a fixed term, say five or ten years. The premiums are level during this period. Premiums for term insurance are quite low when the insured is young, but if you wish to renew the insurance for another five- or ten-year period, you will find that the premiums have risen considerably. In addition, while there are some variations, most term policies will not provide coverage after age 70 or 75. Thus, if your plan requires insurance coverage after this age, you will have to look elsewhere.

Term insurance is most attractive to relatively young people who want to pay as little as possible for the coverage they get.

It is perfect for situations where coverage is needed while the insured is building up his or her estate through retirement planning and investment. This is also the type of coverage you will likely have if you are covered by an insurance plan by your employer or if you have "mortgage" insurance.

As you get older, the premiums may become very high, and if you live beyond the age when you can renew the policy, you will end up with nothing for the premiums you have laid out.

## Whole Life Insurance

The second form of insurance is usually referred to as "whole life" or "permanent" insurance. The premiums are set when you take out the policy and will not vary. Usually they are much higher at the start than premiums for term insurance, but level over the years. As you get older, you will find that these premiums actually become lower in comparison to the premiums for term insurance. This type of policy will stay in force as long as you live and pay the premiums, so it is ideal for planning situations where money will be needed by your family long after you have reached 70. The policy has an "investment" aspect in that a portion of the premiums are invested for the policy owner. (In some cases, this may produce a tax liability.) In many cases, you can "cash in" the policy for money, or you may find that the investment income can be applied to pay annual premiums.

A couple of points should be remembered. First, there is no specific "correct" type of policy when you are choosing between term and whole life. The appropriateness of a policy depends on what your needs are at any particular time. Second, there are an almost infinite variety of options associated with these policies. For example, there may be a provision that if you are disabled, the premiums will be paid for you. Or there may be a provision in a term policy to convert it into whole life. These options may be attractive, but you pay extra for each of them. Third, remember that while the greater majority of insurance agents are reputable professionals, they are paid by commission, and get much more for selling a whole life policy than a term policy. It is important to know what you need. Feel free to shop around among agents until you find one who is willing to discuss your specific needs.

## Other Types of Insurance

Besides life insurance, there are two other types of insurance which you should consider. The first is insurance on your belongings, starting with home-ownership insurance. Most people in Canada under-value their assets, and they would sustain a significant loss, sometimes a crippling one, if their home caught fire. A second type of insurance which should be considered is disability insurance, particularly if you are self-employed. Such insurance will guarantee an income flow to you and your family if you cannot continue to work. Again, there are many variations of this type of insurance, and you should examine the options carefully. While disability insurance is comparatively expensive, if you can afford it, it helps to provide part of a total protection package for your family.

All insurance companies have brochures and pamphlets dealing with the types of insurance they have to offer. It costs nothing to get this type of information which will allow you to make some preliminary decisions as to what type of insurance coverage you need at any particular time and what type of policy gives the best protection at least cost.

# DO SOME TAX PLANNING

At various points in this chapter, we have discussed the tax aspects of various suggested plans, because an important aspect of funding retirement is to save in a way which produces the lowest tax bite. Related to this is an ongoing requirement that you save taxes whenever possible. The less money you pay in taxes, the more you will have available for other purposes. An example of this was the suggestion that you pay down your mortgage before making any other investment, since in most cases, the actual after-tax benefit from this plan is often double what you would get with a more conventional investment.

Reading publications such as *The Financial Post, The Financial Times,* and *The Report on Business* will alert you to more tax-planning and tax-savings ideas. There are also many magazines and books available which are geared to tax savings. Remember that you must always use Canadian publications (since you pay Canadian tax), and you should only rely on up-to-date material since the tax rules change with frightening regularity.

## Income Splitting

There is a form of planning which is basic and which you should always be aware of as you plan your financial affairs. This technique is known as income splitting. In essence, the plan calls for shifting income from one spouse to another. There are a number of reasons why this technique helps you to save tax.

First, you are shifting the tax liability from the spouse with the higher taxes to the spouse with lower taxes. Suppose you earn $35,000 a year and your spouse earns $10,000. If you earn an extra dollar of income, you will pay about 37.5 cents in tax. But if your spouse earned that dollar, he or she would pay only 27 cents. Thus, if you can shift taxes you save more than 10 cents out of each dollar.

Second, there may be a whole range of deductions which your spouse can get which you have already used. For example, suppose you have several thousands of dollars of investment income and several thousands of dollars of pension income. You'll have used your pension and investment income deductions already. But if you could shift $1,000 of investment income plus $1,000 of pension income to your spouse, the family unit will have $2,000 more in deductions.

If you are in a position to employ your spouse and pay a salary, this not only splits income but produces a number of other benefits. Your spouse will be eligible for the annual $500 employment income deduction. By the same token, he or she will be contributing to the Canada or Quebec Pension plans which will result, in due course, in additional income. Eligibility for an RRSP will also open up.

We have already looked at some government-sanctioned income splitting, for this is what the spousal RRSP is. If your spouse has no other private pension source, the spousal RRSP will guarantee an extra $1,000 in pension income deductions when your spouse starts getting an annuity. As we pointed out, you get the same result if your spouse uses a roll-over of the OAS payments to his or her RRSP.

## Attribution Rules

If you want to shift investment income, you must be aware of what are known as the "attribution rules". In a nutshell, if you transfer (give, sell) property to your spouse, any income generated by that property is taxable to you, not your spouse. Thus, if Jones gives Mrs. Jones $10,000 which she invests, the income will be taxable, not to Mrs. Jones, but to Jones himself. (Note, however, that apart from the tax aspects, the income belongs legally to Mrs. Jones.)

The problem can be avoided by lending money. If Jones had loaned Mrs. Jones $10,000, without charging interest, the income generated by the money will be taxable to Mrs. Jones and, if she had no other income, would produce an additional $1,000 investment-income deduction for the couple. To make the loan, all that is required is that Mrs. Jones sign a zero-interest demand note in favour of her husband. (Such a note can be procured at a bank or most stationery stores.) The note simply requires her to repay the money when he asks for it. No interest is to be paid on the loan.

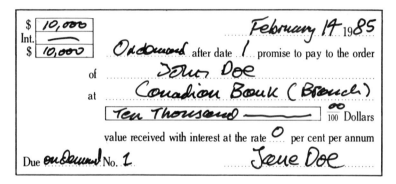

This is the most common way in which to shift investment income from a high-income spouse to one with little or no income.

The technique is also useful in transferring money for the use of minor children, for example, to pay for their education. But in this situation, a trust must be set up because the child cannot legally sign the note. This is not applicable under Quebec law. If you want to explore this type of planning, you should contact a lawyer or institution familiar with tax planning.

Tax aspects should always be a prime consideration before making a major expenditure. For example, a lot of people who have mortgages on their homes also have investments. The interest paid on the mortgage is not deductible. If you sell your investments, you can pay down the mortgage. You can then remortgage the house and use the money to buy investments. If you do this, the interest on the remortgage becomes deductible for tax purposes.

Where you have debts, it is always important to pay off those debts on which interest is non-deductible for tax purposes before paying off debts where interest may be deductible. As a general rule of thumb, if the debt was for personal purposes (such as a mortgage on your home) the interest will not be deductible. But if the debt was for money borrowed for business or investment purposes, it will be deductible.

You should always consider alternative uses for money. Suppose that you have a non-working spouse who has just inherited $10,000. He or she wants a car. You were at the same time planning to invest $10,000. Your spouse should use his or her own money for investment, and you should use your $10,000 to buy the car. By doing things in this fashion, your spouse has the car, but the investment income is taxable at his or her, presumably, lower rate. If you want to retain legal title to the capital, you might arrange to lend your spouse the money for the car, so that you can reclaim "your" $10,000 in the future.

The combination of attention to good investing and good tax planning should help to provide a significant amount of extra income which will make retirement more of a pleasure than it might otherwise have been.

**NOTE:**

In several places in this chapter, we have recommended sources for additional material, including the federal department of Health and Welfare, brokerage houses, insurance companies, and newspapers.

A particularly useful little book entitled *Your Canada Pension Plan* is available through CCH Canadian Limited and is updated every year.

While there are so many good books on investing and tax for the layperson that one hesitates to choose one, an annual book called *Mike Grenby's Tax Tips* (Self-Counsel Press) is the least expensive and the easiest to read in terms of quick pieces of tax advice. However, a trip to your local library will reveal many books on the subject of tax planning, with several new books coming out every year on the topic. Particularly in January and February, you will be able to find low-priced books dealing with RRSPs and how to prepare your tax returns. These latter books often have tax-planning tips incorporated into them. (See "Further Reading" under Drache for additional material.)

# CHAPTER 6

# Leaving it Behind: Estate Planning

*Dying is a very dull, dreary affair. My advice to you is to have nothing whatever to do with it.*

Somerset Maugham
*Last Words* (1965)

B ecause the contemplation of death is an activity enjoyed by few people, it is rarely practised and, unfortunately, even more rarely done in time. However, the ultimate "dull, dreary affair" must be considered when the time comes to draw up a sensible pre-retirement plan. In most people's minds, the term "estate planning" tends to conjure up images of very wealthy people engaging high-priced legal and accounting help to preserve vast amounts of property from taxation. But in reality, most estate planing is undertaken by people of relatively modest means. In essence, the term really applies to the steps you should take to attain three specific goals.

The first of these goals is to provide adequately for those who are dependent upon you in the event that you die or become disabled.

The second is to ensure that the property you own will ultimately go to the people you want to inherit it.

And the third is to minimize the taxes which might otherwise be payable upon your death and which could erode a portion of your assets and perhaps reduce your survivors' standard of living.

Once the objectives of estate planning are understood, it becomes apparent that it is not something which you begin when you are old. The first steps in this form of planning should be undertaken as soon as you have acquired assets or when you first have others dependent upon you. You might, therefore, be in your twenties when you take your first steps, and alter the "plan" as your family and financial circumstances change.

While the term "estate planning" may sound like a grandiose description of what you are trying to do, you should keep in mind that, whatever you call the process, you have an obligation to undertake some very basic steps if you are a responsible person. And the most important of these steps is to make a will.

## WHAT IS A WILL AND WHY DO YOU NEED IT?

A will is a document that tells the people who are in charge of your estate (that is, all the assets which you own or may be entitled to at death) how your assets are to be distributed. The provisions of a will may be very simple or extremely complex, depending upon the nature of your assets and the terms upon which you choose to distribute them.

If you die without a will (known as dying "intestate"), each province has a scheme according to which your assets will be distributed. There are two important reasons why allowing the province to handle distribution is usually unsatisfactory. First, the official scheme of distribution will seldom be the same as you intended. For example, if you die leaving a spouse and children, you might want all your assets to go to your spouse, but the provincial scheme will, in many cases, distribute a portion of your estate to your children.

Second, as we shall see later in this chapter, your estate may be more heavily taxed than if you drew up a will with expert help.

### Why You Need a Lawyer

It is well worth the expense to hire a lawyer to draw up your will. You will find that most lawyers charge very little for doing a will (often just $100 to $150) since wills have traditionally become a type of "loss leader" for legal firms, as the price rarely represents the amount of time put into the job by the lawyer. If you do not have a lawyer, you can contact your provincial law society which will give you the names of lawyers in your area who can draw up a will.

There are a number of reasons why you should use a lawyer. First, the law of wills varies from province to province. Thus, what might be a valid will in one part of Canada may be invalid in another. Consider, for example, a holograph will. This is a will written by the testator (the person making the will) in his or her own handwriting and signed, without a witness. Such a will is valid in many provinces, but not in British Columbia, Prince Edward Island, or Nova Scotia. Other provinces have different rules about how many witnesses you need and who the witnesses can be.

Or consider the situation if you have been divorced. A divorce does not invalidate your will, but in some provinces it may negate gifts made to your ex-spouse. Only a lawyer can explain the effect a divorce may have had on your will in your province. Similarly, you should know that usually a remarriage invalidates an existing will unless you have drawn it up in contemplation of the new marriage. If you have married since you made your last will, it may well be invalid. *You can now see why you should hire a lawyer who is familiar with the laws of your own province.*

There is a second major reason for using a lawyer to draw up your will. Over the centuries, specific language used in wills has taken on precise meanings. If a non-lawyer drafts your will, your heirs may well find that, through the use of inappropriate language, your wishes have not been achieved. Many wills also fail to take into account events which could occur after the will has been drafted. For example, you may well assume, when you leave property to your spouse with the balance to your children, that your spouse will die before your children. But what happens if one child pre-deceases your spouse? Will it make any difference to your objective if that child was married or unmarried? Would the fact that the child who pre-deceases has left a child make any difference? A good will takes into account all contingencies, and a lawyer is trained to consider all the possibilities. As he or she poses the questions, and you answer them, the will becomes complete.

Although a lawyer could make a mistake or put together a "bad" will, the chances of getting exactly what you want in a will drawn up by a lawyer are much better than if a non-lawyer does the job.

## Reviewing Your Will

Most lawyers suggest that you look at your will every three years or so to ensure that it still reflects your wishes. You will find that over a period of time your financial situation will change as well as your family situation. You may find that somebody you wanted to leave property to has since died, or that you have changed your mind about a bequest. A triennial review of your will ensures that it continues to reflect what you really want, and will ensure that future developments are anticipated. *A will should not be drawn on the basis of what you think you might like to happen if you die twenty years from now. Rather, it should be drawn on the basis that you may be hit by a bus just after signing it.*

## The Form of the Will

Although the law does not require that clauses in a will be placed in a specific order, a long-established format exists.

First there will be a clause stating that the document is a will, describing the testator and revoking earlier wills.

The next clause appoints executors and, if necessary, trustees. The role of the executor is usually of fairly short duration. He or she has the obligation to implement the wishes of the testator and deal with the administrative details. These would include paying debts, arranging for burial, identifying and collecting the assets, and then distributing them.

One or more trustees will have to be appointed if you plan to create trusts under your will. Often the trustees will be the same person or people appointed as the executor(s) and we will deal with their selection in the next chapter.

A word about burial. If you have specific wishes about the disposition of your body, that is, interment or cremation, location of burial, dealing with ashes, and so forth, make a point of telling the executor what you want before you die. In many cases, the will is looked at only after burial, and instructions contained in the will may be discovered too late to comply with your wishes.

After the appointment of executors and trustees, there is usually a clause directing the payment of all debts and taxes. Next are the clauses which turn all the assets over to the executor for distribution according to the terms you have set out. If you have one or more trusts, the executor will then turn the property over to the trustees. These provisions are, of course, the key parts of the will.

Following these clauses, there are usually various administrative provisions. The most important of these will give instructions to the executors and trustees as to the ways any assets of the estate are to be invested prior to distribution.

If you have children who are minors, you may want to appoint guardians for them. This is usually done towards the end of the will. It is important to note that a Court will not be bound to accept as guardians the people you name, but normally, great weight is given to the wishes of the testator in this area, so that even though your choice may not be binding in law, it is well worth putting in such a clause. Of course, such a clause would only be effective in the event that both parents were to die, leaving the child or children without a parent.

Once these clauses are in place, the will is signed at the end, according to the requirements of the law of your province.

## Choosing Executors and Trustees

Let's return for a moment to the two items raised earlier: the choice of executors and the use of trusts.

As we mentioned earlier, the executor is charged with looking after the estate and his job may be a relatively short-term one. But if there are trusts in place, the executor will likely be the trustee as well, and may have obligations for an extended period of time. In my experience, one of the most difficult decisions you will have to make in drawing up a will is deciding who should be the executor.

There are a number of considerations. If the will is simple and straightforward with no long-term trusts, picking an executor becomes much easier since the job essentially consists of taking care of debts, getting the assets together, and distributing them. In this situation a spouse, child or other relative is often used as an executor. If you are leaving everything outright to your spouse, it may make sense just to make your spouse the executor.

If, however, there are extensive investments which have to be handled, you should appoint somebody as an executor who is fairly experienced in business matters.

In some cases, especially where trusts have been created for your children, you may want somebody who is familiar with the children, especially if you are giving him or her discretion as to when property will be given to your children.

Finally, you should be aware that you can have groupings of executors or trustees, and allocate specific areas in which they are to act. Thus, if you die with an interest in an operating business, you might appoint your partner as executor to deal only with that business, while somebody else deals with your other assets.

A few technical points should be made. You are not limited to a single executor. You can have as many as you want. But if you have more than one, you want to spell out the rules as to how decisions are made. For example, if you appoint your spouse and a business associate, you may wish to give your spouse the final say on how funds are distributed to your children and the business associate final say on how the assets are to be invested.

Before you appoint an executor, check to make certain that he or she is willing to act. A person cannot be forced to be an executor, and normally is able to resign such an appointment. It is therefore prudent to name alternative executors to replace any who cannot or will not act.

You may also want to give the executors or trustees specific power to hire expert advisors (legal, accounting, investment, or a trust company to hold securities or do bookkeeping) and have the costs charged to the estate. Executors are able to charge for their services, but often when a family member or friend is used no fee will be asked for.

There are several groups from whom executors are drawn, but family members are used most often. As mentioned earlier, a family member is desirable as an executor where personal decisions affecting your survivors may have to be made. The key thing here is to be certain in your own mind that the person selected is capable of handling the job, which in turn may be a function of the nature of your estate and its complexity. The same caution should be taken if you are naming a friend as executor.

When choosing a business associate as an executor, you will have two concerns. First, you must be satisfied that he or she will have time to do the job right. Second, if you and the associate have business interests in common, the executor may find that this role puts him or her in a conflict of interest between what is best for the estate and what is best for him or her as a business person.

*If you are considering lawyers or accountants as executors, the key concern is whether they will have time to do the job properly.*

Often, a good choice of executor is a trust company, but there are three potential drawbacks. First, if the estate is not large, many trust companies do not feel it is worthwhile to take on this role. Second, a trust company will definitely charge its fees to the estate. Third, trust companies tend to be conservative in investing and will not particularly wish to get involved in personal decision-making relating to the family.

In your particular situation, it may be obvious who should be your executor. But it is always worthwhile to remember that you can "mix and match" executors, so that the broad level of expertise to handle your estate is always available.

## Creating a Trust

We have referred many times already to the creation of trusts under a will. Basically, a trust is created when you instruct your executor to set aside assets for one or more particular purposes, as opposed to making an immediate distribution. In such a case, unless you appoint someone else as "trustee" (the person who deals with the trust property), your executor will likely be the trustee. His or her obligation as trustee is to invest the assets and then to distribute the income and capital as instructed.

While trusts may be of an almost unlimited variety, the most common are designed to protect the assets of people who are not able to deal with them properly, usually because of age but sometimes because of physical or mental disability.

Suppose you have two children, now eight and ten. You want to provide for them in your will, but you certainly do not want them to get the money at too early an age. You can set up a trust under your will containing the terms you wish to impose. For example, you can tell your trustee to invest the money and accumulate the income until the children reach age 25, at which time each child gets his or her share. But you might also say that if the child needs money for education before that time, the trustee can advance the needed funds. At this juncture, you either give discretion to advance the funds to the trustee alone, or name somebody else (say the guardian of the children) or create some other mechanism which will tell the trustee when funds are to be advanced.

This simple example shows how a trust works. While trusts for children are the most common, occasionally there are trusts for spouses (income to my spouse for life, capital to children upon the death of the spouse), trusts for charity, or for many other purposes.

The key reason for setting up a trust is to prevent the immediate distribution of property and, in many cases, to set conditions before the property is distributed. If you do create a trust under your will, and a very large percentage of wills do so, the obligations of the trustee (executor) may extend for many years. Obviously, therefore, the selection of the right person or group of people is crucial.

We shall look at trusts again later in this chapter when we discuss various tax-planning options.

## WHERE A WILL IS NOT APPLICABLE

A will is important where you have property to pass along to another person, but you should be aware that there are certain types of property which do not pass by will. In addition, there are some limitations about what you can do under your will, which will vary from province to province. The following is a list of property which passes without a will.

**1. Insurance:** If you have taken out an insurance policy and named an individual as a beneficiary, the insurance proceeds will go directly to the named person on your death and will not form part of your estate. If, however, you name your estate as beneficiary of the policy, the funds come into your estate and are disposed of in accordance with your will.

**2. Pension Income:** In the vast majority of cases, entitlement to a pension out of a pension plan, deferred profit-sharing plan, or registered retirement savings plan, passes to the individual whom you designated when you became a member of the plan. Many lawyers, however, do suggest that the designation under the plan be reinforced through a clause inserted in your will.

**3. Gifts:** If you have made a gift prior to your death, the property you gave away is no longer yours, and thus does not pass under your will.

**4. Life Interests:** You may have the use of property only so long as you are alive. For example, your spouse may have died, leaving you the family home for as long as you live, and indicating that it is to pass to a child when you die. You have a "life interest" in the home but have no right to transfer it by your will.

**5. Jointly Owned Property:** If you own a property jointly with someone else, the other person will automatically own the property when you die. Thus if you and your spouse are joint owners of the family home and have joint bank accounts, upon the death of one of you the other gets the whole of the joint property without it passing through the estate. (This does not apply, however, under Quebec law.)

**6. Property Subject to a Sales Agreement:** Occasionally a person dies after having agreed to sell property to someone else. If such an agreement exists the executor will be legally bound to carry through with the sale. Thus, the property will not become part of the estate, though the proceeds from the sale probably will.

In addition to the above exceptions to the general rule, you should be aware that there are some other limitations. For example, if you leave money for a purpose which is against public policy (e.g., to a seditious organization) the clause will not be legally effective.

And now, in most provinces, there is legislation, usually related to matrimonial law, which requires the deceased to provide for a surviving spouse and other dependents. If you leave all your assets to a home for stray cats and nothing to your spouse or dependent children, an application can be made to the courts to set aside funds from your estate for the support of your dependents. The actual rules vary from province to province, but you should be aware that nowhere in Canada can you shirk your responsibilities to those who are dependent upon you. You should check with your lawyer to see who falls into such a category in your province, and what guidelines can be suggested if you want to leave the minimum amount.

## A Few Final Points

If you want to amend your will in some relatively minor way, it can be done through making a "codicil", a short amending statement. Again, a lawyer should be consulted, because there are technical rules which must be followed for the codicil to be valid.

A will may be revoked at any time and a new one substituted for it. As we mentioned, this is usually formally done at the beginning of any will. A will usually is revoked if it is destroyed with the intention of revoking it, but not if it is accidentally destroyed, as in a fire. In Quebec, revocation by destruction is more complex, and you must also destroy any copy held by the notary who drew it. And, as we noted in passing earlier, in most cases a marriage will automatically revoke a will but this is not applicable under Quebec law.

Anybody can make a will provided he or she is 18 years of age (or younger if in the armed forces) and of sound mind. Often, in the case of older people who may be hospitalized, it becomes a question (which sometimes leads to litigation) whether they understood what they were doing when they made a will.

Finally, what do you do with the will once you have it? Usually there are two choices. You can leave it with your lawyer who will keep it safe, giving you a "true copy" for your records. Conversely, you may keep the original will, which should be placed in a safe deposit box. You should inform your executors as to where the will may be found, since a lengthy delay in finding the will may cause hardship in your family because your assets cannot be distributed.

We have only touched on the highlights of will-making and the various things which can (or should) be done in a will in this section, in order to familiarize the reader with the process so that when he or she goes to see a lawyer it will be done with a basic grasp of what the will should contain and with a good idea of the types of information (executors, trustees, guardians, lists of assets, and so forth) which will have to be provided.

## TAXATION AT DEATH

Neither Canadian provinces (with the exception of Quebec) nor the Federal Government impose death duties directly. (The Quebec situation is discussed at the end of this chapter.) But there are a number of rules in the Income Tax Act which trigger tax liability upon death, and these must be considered in the context of your estate planning.

Upon death, the basic rule is that you are deemed to have disposed of all your capital assets (stocks, bonds, real estate) immediately before you died. If the assets are non-depreciable (that is, the types of assets on which capital cost allowance is not claimed, such as stocks), you are treated as having sold them at fair market value. If the assets are depreciable (say, a building you owned and rented out), the disposition is deemed to take place at the mid-point between the cost for tax purposes (original cost minus depreciation claimed) and fair market value. But while the deemed disposition theoretically may apply to the home you live in, no tax will normally be payable at death because it is a principal residence and produces a tax-free gain.

The same deemed disposition rules apply if you leave the country permanently, so that if you are planning to retire to some other country, you should also bear these rules in mind.

Let's look at a couple of examples. Suppose you bought 1,000 shares of Consolidated Moose Pasture for $10 each. When you die, they are worth $15. You would have been deemed to have disposed of the shares for $15, and when your final-year tax return is prepared (covering the period from January 1 until the day you died) a $5,000 capital gain would have to be reported.

What about depreciable property? Suppose you bought a house for $100,000 and have rented it out since you acquired it. Over the years you claimed $20,000 in depreciation, so its tax cost (known as the undepreciated capital cost, or UCC) is $80,000. Suppose you die when the house is worth $150,000. You will have been deemed to have disposed of the house for $115,000 (the mid-point between $80,000 and $150,000) with the following tax results: The difference between $80,000 and $100,000 (the original purchase price) is "recaptured", that is, added back into income. The additional $15,000 is a capital gain and one-half of this is added into income. Thus, in the tax return submitted after your death, in addition to any other income which must be reported, $27,500 in respect of the rental house will have to be reported.

*Obviously, a fair amount of planning must be done to cope with the big tax bite on death.*

## HOW TO MINIMIZE THE TAX BITE

Happily, there are a number of roll-overs available. In the chapter dealing with financial planning for retirement, we discussed a number of roll-overs which had the effect of deferring taxation in respect of certain types of income. In this context, we are discussing roll-overs which deal with the transfer of capital assets.

The most important of these roll-overs for a married person is the so-called spousal roll-over. This provision allows you to transfer property on your death to your spouse and avoid the tax liability at death.

Suppose that in our example with the Consolidated Moose

Pasture shares, you left the shares to your spouse. Instead of having a $5,000 capital gain to report, no tax will be payable. Instead, your spouse will take the shares at your original cost, $10,000. No tax liability will apply to the shares until your spouse actually sells the shares or dies.

The same thing will happen if you leave your rental house to your spouse. In this case, the spouse would take the house with your adjusted cost base ($100,000) and your UCC of $80,000. The tax liability which may attach will only apply when the house is sold or your spouse dies.

The spousal roll-over is one reason why the most common of simple wills in Canada simply provides that everything go to the spouse of the testator. Usually, where this is to be done, the bequest is conditional on the spouse's surviving the testator by 30 or 60 days so that if they die in a common accident, the property never enters the spouse's estate but passes directly to whomever is to get it if the spouse is not alive at the death of the original testator.

## A Spouse Trust

There is another alternative which is popular. You may want to ensure that your spouse has the use of all your property but you really want it to go, after his or her death, to your children. In this case, what you need is a spouse trust. The roll-over applies on a transfer of property to a spouse trust, which is a trust which provides that nobody but the spouse has a right to any of the income or capital while the spouse is alive.

So, you can leave all your property to your spouse and instruct the trustees that the spouse is to receive the income. If you so desire, you can allow him or her to draw down capital if it is needed. Upon the death of the spouse, you simply indicate that the balance of the funds are to go, say, to your children in equal shares.

However, there is a trap for the unwary. If you put in a clause which says that the trust will terminate if the spouse remarries, the trust will not qualify as a spouse trust since somebody other than the spouse can get the funds before the death of the spouse, and the roll-over will not apply. Therefore, you must make a decision between the tax deferral associated with such a trust and your desire not to fund your spouse's second marriage.

There are other roll-overs. For example, if you transfer farm property or shares in a farming corporation to a child or grandchild who continues to farm the property, the heir will take it at your tax cost, and capital gains and recapture will be deferred indefinitely.

## The $200,000 Roll-Over

One of the most important roll-overs for those who carry on business through a private company is known as the $200,000 roll-over. If you transfer shares in a private company which carries on an active business (or a company which only holds shares in such a company) there is a deferral of up to $200,000 of capital gains if the shares go to a child or grandchild.

Suppose you own all 1,000 shares of OPCO, a company which manufactures widgets. The shares have a tax cost of $100,000 and are worth $500,000. If you die and leave the shares to your child, the fair market value of the shares for tax purposes is reduced by up to $200,000 of capital gain. Thus, instead of the shares going at $500,000, they are deemed to be transferred at $300,000. Instead of having a $400,000 capital gain at your death, the gain is just $200,000. But your child will take the shares at a tax cost of $300,000, which means that when he or she sells the shares or dies, the additional capital gains tax will be payable, unless, of course, the child also uses the roll-over.

But it is possible to double the exemption if you draw your will carefully. Suppose you left just 500 of the shares to your child. These would be worth $250,000 and your tax cost for 500 shares would be $50,000. You get the $200,000 roll-over, so no tax is payable in respect of these shares. You then leave the other 500 shares to your spouse outright. (For technical reasons, they cannot be left to a spousal trust.) Your spousal roll-over ensures that no tax is payable. Then your spouse can either gift the shares or leave them under his or her will to the child, using the spouse's $200,000 roll-over. This is possible because everybody is entitled to $200,000 of roll-over under this provision during his or her lifetime.

Clearly, if you want to do something like this, a lot of care should be given to the drafting of the appropriate clauses in the will.

## Division of Assets for Taxation Purposes

Because some assets will trigger tax liability and others will not, when you draw your will, you should either specify who gets what, or give your executor wider discretion in the distribution of property.

For example, suppose your estate is worth $500,000, and includes some real estate which carries both potential recapture and capital gains, shares in your business, the family home and some other stocks which are up in value. You want to split the estate between your spouse and child, fifty-fifty. If you give your child the real estate and the appreciated shares which are not from your own company, capital gains liability and recapture will ensue. On the other hand, if you give the child the family home and/or the shares in the family company, there will be no tax liability. Therefore, the division of assets should take into account the tax effect of distributing particular assets to particular heirs. Since this is often impractical when you draw the will because you have no idea of what assets you may be holding when you die and how much they may have appreciated, you should indicate the percentage split between various heirs and instruct the executor to distribute assets among the heirs, bearing in mind the tax consequences.

Since there are a number of "elections" which an executor may make under the Income Tax Act, it is also prudent to include a clause giving the executor the specific power to make tax elections. This is most important where there are trusts for infant children, since elections can be made which minimize the taxes which might otherwise be payable by the trusts.

## Spousal Wills

In many situations, only one spouse makes a will. Traditionally, the man has control of the assets and often the wife has very little in her own name. But the wife should very definitely have a will. Since, in most cases, the wife will be a major beneficiary under her husband's will, it is prudent for her to have a will, even if she has no substantial assets when it is drawn. This covers the eventuality that the wife dies soon after the husband, having inherited the assets but not having had time to draw up her own will.

## Gifting

Up to now, we have focused on the disposition of assets under a will. But as we pointed out earlier, one of the objects of estate planning is to ensure that specific property goes to a specific person. While this can be done by will, there is an element of greater certainty if you gift the property while you are alive.

There are some pros and cons to this approach.

One of the major "pluses" is that, by gifting, you can ensure that property or money goes to somebody when that person needs it most. For example, suppose you planned to leave each of your children $25,000 in your will. One of the kids is buying a house and mortgage rates are high. It might be much better from the child's point of view if you gave him or her the $25,000 now, when it is needed, rather than, say, twenty years from now when you die and the house has been paid for with after-tax dollars.

Obviously, you can only do this sort of thing if you have the cash available and are reasonably certain of your own financial health without the $25,000.

When you make a gift, you should recognize that you cannot change your mind. Once the property has been transferred to the donee (as the recipient is known in law), you have no right to it again and cannot demand it back. This may be contrasted with a bequest under a will, where you can change your mind up until your death.

Gifting is often used to make charitable donations. Where a large gift is made, the tax rules are more generous with regard to deducting the gift when you are alive than if the gift is left by will. If you make the gift while you are alive, you can claim the deduction over a period of up to six years, while a gift by will qualifies for a deduction for only two years.

Charitable gifts made while you are alive will also allow you to bask in the warm reception you will receive for making the gift, which may be an important consideration.

You may also want to use a trust in a gifting situation. For example, you may wish to give $50,000 for the use of your young grandchildren but at the same time want to ensure that they do not get their hands on the money before they reach age 21. You can create a trust and gift the money to the trust, providing for income to be used for the benefit of the children and the capital distributed when they reach age 21. (For reasons which are discussed below relating to tax, the most common use of a trust entails a loan of money to the trust for the infant children, which may be converted into a gift after they reach age 18.)

Gifting should be considered in two main situations. First, if you have specific personal property (e.g., art or jewellery) which you wish somebody to have, a gift may be an appropriate way of transferring it. Second, if you are financially secure, gifting money or property when you are alive may be attractive from the point of view of reducing your current taxes (if you gift shares, the dividends will be taxed to the donee) and ensuring they have funds when the money is most needed.

## Tax Aspects of Gifting

There are no gift taxes in Canada, except in Quebec, but once again, there are general tax rules which will apply.

First, when you gift property, you are deemed to have disposed of it at fair market value, which may trigger a capital gain liability. Unlike the case of a bequest, even depreciable property will be deemed to have been disposed of at fair market value, not the mid-point between UCC and fair market value. Thus, normally one does not gift depreciable property but leaves it by will.

Second, we have the income attribution rules. In a nutshell, these require that where income is generated by gifted property, and the gift has been made to a spouse or to a person who at the time the income is generated is under age 18, the income is taxable to the donor, not the donee. This, of course, discourages gifting of income-producing property (and this includes money if it is used for investment) between spouses and to young children. But this rule does not apply to money which is loaned, and it is for this reason we noted above that where a trust is set up for young children, the money is often loaned to the trust. Once the children reach age 18, the loan can be forgiven, and the income-attribution rules will not apply.

(In Quebec, a loan of money may trigger the possibility of gift tax. This will be discussed later in this chapter.)

But again, there are exceptions to the deemed disposition rules. Any property transferred to a spouse will go to the spouse at the donor's tax cost. However, any capital gain which arises when the spouse sells the property will be attributed back to the donor.

If you were to gift your home to somebody, while there is a deemed realization, the principal residence rules would protect you from taxation. Thus, if you are moving to an apartment and your child might like the old family home, it can be gifted without a capital gains problem emerging.

Gifts of personal property, furniture, clothes, jewellery, stamps, coins, art, and so forth are deemed to have a tax cost of $1,000. Thus, any gift of personal property with a fair market value of less than $1,000 will produce no capital gain.

And the roll-over we discussed earlier, relating to farm property and the shares in a small business corporation apply equally to gifts made while you are alive as well as to bequests at death. If you are gifting property to a charity to be used directly in its own work, such as a painting to an art gallery, an election can be made which can, if you desire, eliminate capital gains taxes on the gift.

If you are going to make any major gifts, you had best consult a lawyer or an accountant before the gift is made to ensure that, from a tax point of view, you do not run into any nasty surprises. But, tax problems aside, gifting is often a key element in estate planning and should be given serious consideration.

## SOME ESTATE PLANNING IDEAS

Up to now in this chapter, we have discussed a number of the basic factors which are involved in estate planning, along with some ideas which have fairly broad general applications. However, estate planning is an intensely personalized exercise. What may be ideal for one person will be totally inappropriate for another. The key variables are:

**1.** The family situation, with an emphasis on the dependents and their potential needs.

**2.** The amount of assets which are subject to planning.

**3.** The income flow for the family. In this context, we can distinguish between, for example, a millionaire who has relatively low income from investments in raw land and a person with very little in the way of savings but a substantial annual income from salary and retirement funds.

**4.** The nature of the assets in the estate.

**5.** Future plans including the possibility of a widow or widower remarrying, retiring outside of Canada, or starting a second business after retirement.

**6.** An estimation of the effect of inflation both on one's needs and on the increase in the nominal value of one's assets.

7. Ongoing business relationships with non-family members.

Clearly these and other factors will help decide the nature of an estate plan. It should be abundantly clear that where there are substantial assets involved, it is imperative that professional advice be sought, not just in terms of drawing up a will, but for tax minimization, creating trusts and a myriad of other aspects involved in actually implementing an estate plan. It also follows that no single book, much less a chapter in a book, can canvass all planning possibilities. But in the following pages, we'll look at a few planning points which may be of importance to those with substantial assets.

## The Estate Freeze

One of the most important estate planning tools available to those who have enough resources to maintain themselves for the rest of their lives is known as the "estate freeze". In essence, what this plan does is stop the growth of one's assets at the time the freeze is implemented and shift the growth to somebody else, most usually to one or more children. The following is a simple example of a freeze.

Suppose that you own a building which cost you $250,000 and is now worth $500,000. Its UCC is $150,000. You have enough assets to live on comfortably. You also believe the building will appreciate in value over the next ten years, say to $750,000.

If you simply retain the building and it rises in value as you predicted, the increase will mean an additional $250,000 capital gain for you, either on the sale of the building or if you should die.

But you could sell the building to your children today for $500,000. This would produce immediate income tax consisting of $100,000 in recapture and $250,000 in capital gains. (If the sale is subject to a mortgage back, the capital gain can be spread over a number of years.) The key is that if the building does rise to $750,000 in value, the additional capital gain of $250,000 is taxable to your children, not to you. In addition the tax on this extra gain will be payable only when the children die or sell the building, thus deferring the tax bite. What you have done is to "freeze" the value for your estate-planning purposes as of today's date and shifted the future gain to your children whom, presumably, you would want to inherit the building anyway.

The most common form of estate freeze is often associated

with shares in a family-owned company. Suppose you own all the shares of OPCO which have a value now of $800,000 and a tax cost of $100,000. You want to retire from the business and turn it over to the children. You also feel that the shares will rise rapidly in value. And you want to keep voting control. You take the following steps:

**1.** You create a new company, called HOLDCO.

**2.** You transfer your shares of OPCO to HOLDCO for preferred shares of HOLDCO worth $800,000, the value of your OPCO shares.

**3.** For tax purposes, this is not considered to be a taxable transaction, but the cost of your preferred shares is just $100,000, the same as the OPCO shares which you transferred. (You'll recognize this transaction as a roll-over.)

**4.** The HOLDCO preferred shares pay you a dividend of, say, 8 per cent a year, giving you a cash flow of $64,000 in dividends. The shares are voting.

**5.** The children subscribe for a nominal amount of HOLDCO shares, each getting, say, 10 shares for $1 apeice. This low price is appropriate since all the value of HOLDCO shares is in the preference shares you own.

But given this corporate structure, if HOLDCO rises in value, the preference shares will not increase in value. Rather the common shares will go up. In other words, you have shifted all future growth to the children who hold the common shares. (Since OPCO is fully owned by HOLDCO, any increase in OPCO's value automatically is reflected in the HOLDCO shares.)

In addition, the preference shares you hold qualify for the $200,000 capital gains roll-over. This means that you can, either by gift or will, transfer a portion of your preference shares to your children and still get a tax advantage. And, as was pointed out in the discussion of will planning, it is possible to double-up on the $200,000 roll-over.

The above-mentioned freeze is a sort of tax classic, known to almost anybody who does any tax work. There is a range of variations which can be built in. If you don't want control, you make the preference shares non-voting. If you want to draw salary income you can be employed by OPCO under a management contract.

If you want your grandchildren to share in the growth, you can set up a trust and have the trust buy some of the HOLDCO common shares.

The key point is that you have effectively frozen your position for tax purposes and shifted future growth to those whom you would benefit.

There are many ways of setting up such a freeze, of which the two examples mentioned are the most common. If you plan to investigate this planning technique, expert assistance is vital, since the expert will, among other things, canvass other freeze plans with you.

Several additional points should be borne in mind:

**1.** You do not enter into a freeze unless you are financially comfortable.

**2.** When the freeze is set up, you should know whether you need an income flow from the new arrangement, how you want to receive income, and whether you are prepared to give up or retain voting control.

**3.** Be careful about selecting the beneficiaries of the freeze. It is very difficult and often very expensive to undo a freeze.

**4.** A freeze is seldom done in favour of a spouse since the full roll-over provisions obviate the need for freezing in a spouse's favour.

**5.** If you are freezing a business, consider whether it is appropriate to benefit all your children through a freeze. If only one or two are to work in the business, having the others as equal shareholders who do not have to work may be a mistake. Consider giving an ongoing business only to those who will operate it, with an equivalent value going to the other children out of other assets. If there are no other assets, insurance in favour of the children who do not operate the business might be appropriate.

## ESTATE PLANNING: DEALING WITH NON-FAMILY BUSINESS ASSOCIATES

It is very common for people in business to have associates who are not related to them. They may have partners or be shareholders in a particular enterprise. Estate planning revolving around business relationships with a non-related person can be very difficult, but is absolutely essential.

Consider a situation where Brown and Green started a business twenty years ago. They each own 50 per cent of the shares of BG Enterprises. The business is flourishing, and the initial investment of each of them, $10,000, is now worth more than $50,000. Each one works full time in the business and each concentrates in a special area of expertise.

What happens if one of the partners dies?

Let's look at what happens if no particular estate planning is done. Suppose Brown dies and, in order to defer any tax liability, leaves all his shares to a spouse. The first question is whether the spouse is willing and able to take on Brown's responsibility in the business. In most cases, the answer is no. The next question is whether Green is prepared to do the work of two and still share the profits equally with Brown's spouse. Again, the answer may be no. If BG Enterprises has to hire a person to do Brown's work, should the cost of paying this person be borne by the company (which means in effect Brown's spouse and Green) equally, or should the cost be somehow charged only to Brown's spouse? Does Brown leave any children who might come into the business and eventually assume Brown's role? If there are children, is Green willing to work with them?

These are the basic questions, though there are others which might be considered. What if one of the two becomes disabled for an extended period of time and cannot work? What happens if they have a basic disagreement about running the company which cannot be resolved?

## Partnership and Shareholder Agreements

The answers to all these questions lie in negotiation which ideally should take place right at the start of their working relationship. It is essential that where two or more people work together in an enterprise, they should have a written agreement which deals with all these issues, as well as such matters as how decisions are made, who will be directors and officers, how much each will get in remuneration and under what circumstances profits will be distributed. In the case of partners, such agreements are called "partnership agreements" and where they are involved in a corporation, the agreements are called "shareholder agreements" or "buy-sell agreements". Without such an agreement, trouble will inevitably loom when death or disability arises.

Obviously, what is in any particular agreement will depend to a great degree on the specific situation and the answers to the various questions posed above.

But such an agreement should at the very least incorporate provisions for dealing with the business in three key situations: death, disability, or a falling out between the associates.

# 1. The Death of a Business Partner

The first decision clearly is whether the survivor of the two associates is willing to have the family members of the deceased remain as shareholders. Where the business is on the small side and each of the two founders puts in a lot of personal work to ensure the success of the enterprise, usually it is impractical to assume that after the death of one, the other will work to support the deceased's family. On the other hand, if the business is a very large one and the input of the founders had become basically managerial, letting the family of the deceased stay on as shareholders may be acceptable, especially if there are children who may come into the business.

If the arrangement is that, upon death, control of the business should go to the survivor, then you will want a mandatory buy-sell provision in the agreement. Such a provision would require the surviving founder to buy all the shares held by the deceased. It is usual to set a formula in the agreement to fix the purchase price and to set out how the purchase will be funded. The shares might be paid for over time, or, as is more common, the agreement may require each of the founders to insure the other, so that, when one dies, the other gets the insurance money (tax free) which will be used to buy the shares held by the deceased.

It is beyond the scope of this book to go into the many variables. In some cases, the insurance is owned by the company while in other cases, each of the founders personally owns the insurance on the other. In some cases the sale is made by the estate of the deceased, while in others, the shares have been transferred to beneficiaries who then sell. Where the corporation owns the insurance, the transaction may take place through the company redeeming the shares for cancellation, effectively vesting full control in the survivor.

There are different tax and business aspects associated with each variation and expert advice should be sought at the time the agreement is made to determine what is best in the particular circumstances. An insurance agent should be used as an adviser on the nature of the insurance (which usually will be whole-life) and a lawyer or an accountant familiar with the tax aspects should also be consulted.

## 2. Disability of a Business Partner

The agreement should come to grips with what happens if one of the founders becomes disabled and cannot work. The first thing to deal with is the definition of disability, which will relate in part to the time during which the person cannot work. Usually, for example, the provisions dealing with disability will not apply until one of the parties has been unable to work for three or six months. Thus, a relatively short-term illness or injury will not trigger the provision.

The agreement may call for the non-disabled party to buy out the disabled one. Here, spelling out the terms of the financing are particularly important since life insurance cannot be relied upon for funding. Usually, the disability provision provides for a buy-out over a fairly lengthy period of time to allow the business to generate the needed income. Some agreements do not call for a buy-out but will deny the disabled person the right to salary, substituting instead disability payments. Such payments are then usually covered by taking out disability insurance in respect of the two parties.

While we have discussed situations where there are just two parties, the comments made in these pages apply equally to situations where there are three or more people involved. In such cases, the agreements are similar but more complex.

## 3. Irreconcilable Differences Between Business Partners

While nobody enters into a business arrangement with the thought that there may eventually be a big fight with the associates, it happens often enough so that the situation should be taken into account.

A common arrangement exists known as the "shotgun clause". Under this scheme, if one of the parties is unhappy with the other, he or she tenders an offer to buy the other person's shares, setting out the price and the terms. The person to whom the offer is tendered then has the option of selling his or her shares on those terms or buying the shares from the tendering party on the same terms. This procedure is designed to ensure that the tendering party makes a fair offer, since he or she cannot know in advance whether he or she will be a buyer or a seller.

In a situation such as this, terms for financing are not set out in the agreement itself, but rather in the "tender". Clearly, the person who "triggers the shotgun" will only make an offer at a price and upon terms which he can meet.

*The best time to make a partnership or shareholder agreement is when the parties embark on their joint enterprise, but it is never too late. If you have a business arrangement with a non-family member and there is no such agreement, you should make this a high priority.*

It should be clear that in making such an arrangement, you are taking a crucial step in terms of estate planning, since each party will then know just what will happen if he or she dies owning shares in the company. From an estate-planning point of view, this is important for several reasons. First, if the shares have appreciated in value substantially, they may form the bulk of your estate but may not generate a lot of cash. Second, shares in private companies may be very hard to sell to anybody other than the shareholder(s). This means that you may have shares worth hundreds of thousands of dollars which cannot readily be converted into cash. The mandatory buy-sell arrangement copes with this problem. And third, with a mandatory buy-sell you know what cash will be available for your family on death, and thus can do your additional planning, confident that your key asset has been dealt with in a manner satisfactory to you.

While we have stressed the need for these types of arrangements where there is a non-family business associate, in many family businesses the same arrangements are used. While there may be ties of blood or marriage, you can readily understand that if a business is run by two or three brothers, there may be identical questions posed when one brother dies and the heirs (and potential business associates) are a sister-in-law or nieces and nephews.

In the following section, we'll take a brief look at the use of insurance in estate planning, a subject which has been touched on already in earlier pages and in the chapter dealing with financial planning for retirement.

## LIFE INSURANCE AND ESTATE PLANNING

In the chapter on financial planning, we looked at the basic types of life insurance: term insurance and whole life (or permanent) insurance. We pointed out that the type of insurance bought would be a function of its purpose, and in many cases, term insurance would be the most appropriate type. But when we look at estate planning, the important thing about insurance is that it be available always, no matter what the age of the insured. This suggests that, in most cases, whole life insurance may be required for estate-planning purposes.

In the foregoing pages we have already mentioned a number of situations where insurance will be important in estate planning. The following list suggests some other uses and will remind you of those previously mentioned:

## Liquidity

In many cases, a person may be wealthy without having a lot of assets which can readily be turned into cash. If you are a millionaire and all your money is tied up in real estate which cannot be quickly sold, your estate may need "instant cash" to meet debts, the living expenses of your survivors, taxes, and so forth. Insurance can be used to provide funds for the estate or heirs until your other property can be sold.

## Taxes

As we have pointed out, significant tax liabilities can arise on death. Insurance may be extremely useful in providing cash to meet these liabilities, eliminating the need to sell property to raise money. An important aspect should be noted. If you use roll-overs to defer tax, consider who should be insured. For example, if your will calls for all your assets to go to your spouse on death, there will be no tax when you die, but there may be a very substantial tax liability when your spouse dies. In this situation, insurance should be taken out on the life of the spouse, with the beneficiaries being the spouse's estate or the heirs under the spouse's will.

## Key Man Insurance

If you are running a business which you hope to pass along to your children, but the children are too young to take over, key man insurance may be an option to consider. The company insures your life. If you die, the insurance is payable to the company which then uses it to hire one or more people to replace you. They will run the business and train your children until they can take over. This is obviously a simplified example of the use of such insurance in that there may be real difficulties in finding the right person, but a fund of tax-free money coming to the company may give your family the opportunity to hire an extremely skilled manager to replace you if need be.

## Debt Insurance

If you have significant debts, which may be associated with your business or other assets, insurance may be purchased and earmarked for the liquidation of outstanding loans. Many people, most notably professionals, underestimate the amount of debt they have outstanding at any time through overdraft financing of their business through the bank. While the financing can be handled easily while you are around and working, it could become extremely onerous if you should die and your income flow disappears.

As a general observation, we might point out that few people like to buy insurance, just as most people tend to shy away from making wills. But experience shows that very few, other than the wealthy, can put together a coherent estate plan while ignoring the importance of insurance. As was pointed out, usually you will want permanent insurance in connection with an estate plan; and it is stressed that, over the long haul, this type of insurance is cheapest when bought at an early age. Thus, prudence indicates that considering your insurance requirements should be a high and early priority in terms of estate planning.

## QUEBEC GIFT TAX AND SUCCESSION DUTIES

It has been pointed out earlier that only Quebec retains gift taxes and imposes taxes on death, through its Succession Duty Act. If you live in Quebec or have substantial property there, you should be generally familiar with the rules. However, it should be stressed that only an overview of the law can be given here, and you should discuss these acts with a lawyer, notary, or accountant in Quebec before taking any major steps in respect of estate planning.

It should also be pointed out that, while these acts have to be considered, the "federal" rules which have already been discussed also apply in Quebec. Occasionally, you will find a conflict between a tax planning idea which is tax-free federally but which may produce a tax liability in Quebec.

# The Quebec Gift Tax

The Quebec gift tax is imposed on individuals or trusts resident in Quebec who make gifts. It also applies to a non-resident of Quebec if he or she makes a gift of real estate situated in the province, even if the recipient of the gift is a non-resident. Thus, the gift tax rules will often apply to gifts of, say, a cottage in Quebec, even if a resident of Ontario gives the cottage to a resident of British Columbia.

The rate of tax is a flat 20 per cent of the gift, but there are some basic exemptions.

First, you can make up to five gifts a year to individuals (and a trust is considered an individual) of up to $5,000 apiece. But remember that if you give one child $6,000 and another $4,000, you will have to pay tax on $1,000, since one of the gifts exceeded $5,000 by that amount.

You can also make a once-in-a-lifetime gift of up to $300,000 if the property gifted is farm property going to a child.

If there is more than one beneficiary under a trust, the exemption of $5,000 will not apply. This means that if you are planning to set up a trust and gift (or lend, as we shall see) money to it, each trust must have just one beneficiary. This may create some technical difficulties if you want to benefit all your children or grandchildren.

All gifts to a spouse or to a spouse trust are free of tax as are gifts to charitable organizations.

Small gifts, those under $100, can be made without limitation.

It should be noted that most gifts can be doubled up. Suppose you want to give your child $10,000 in a year. You could make a gift of $5,000 to the child and $5,000 to your spouse. The spouse in turn can make a $5,000 gift to the child.

The Gift Tax Act deems a number of transactions to be gifts for tax purposes, though they are not gifts as a matter of law. Most of these "deemed gifts" are rather arcane (such as the renunciation of a right you have to property in favour of some-body else) but one is extremely important in the context of a number of tax-planning ideas we have discussed. This is the rule which states that where an interest-free or low-interest loan is made to a person to whom you are related, a deemed gift arises. The gift is deemed to be the amount of the loan multiplied by a "prescribed rate", which varies from time to time. At the time of writing, the prescribed rate is 11 per cent.

Suppose you lend $10,000 to your child as part of an income-splitting plan. You would be deemed to have made a gift of $10,000 × 0.11 or $1,100. Since this is less than your $5,000 exemption, no tax would be payable. But tax liability will apply when the amount of the loan exceeds about $45,000.

A loan to a wife is not affected by this provision since gifts between spouses are not taxable.

But a loan to a trust which has more than one beneficiary will be fully taxable, since the $5,000 exemption is not available.

Another point should be remembered. We discussed a number of roll-overs to children as part of estate planning. For Quebec income-tax purposes, the roll-overs are the same as under the federal rules. But with the exception of the $300,000 exemption for farm properties mentioned earlier, which is being changed by an amendment now before the Quebec National Assembly, a gift which utilizes the roll-overs may still be taxable under the Gift Tax Act. Professional advice should be sought before any major gift is contemplated, even if the income-tax provisions allow for a roll-over.

It should be recognized that the Gift Tax Act is not a terribly important statute, but it is designed to help "protect" the Succession Duty Act. In the absence of the Gift Tax Act, residents of Quebec would simply give their property away before death, avoiding the death tax. We shall now look at the effect of the Succession Duty Act.

## The Quebec Succession Duty Act

The Quebec Succession Duty Act imposes a tax on those who inherit property, not on the estate of the deceased. It applies only to deaths which occur after April 19, 1978; another act deals with deaths which occurred prior to that date.

There are two main "charging" sections. The first imposes tax where property situated within Quebec is "transmitted" as a consequence of somebody's death. This would apply, of course, to a situation where a person residing outside of Quebec owned Quebec-based property.

The second charging provision applies in situations where a person residing or domiciled in Quebec receives property situated outside Quebec as a consequence of death. This means that if you have any heirs in Quebec, although you live outside the province, the tax may apply on your death.

There is a series of exemptions and deductions under the Act. The first applies to situations where the heir is the spouse of the deceased. In such a case, no tax will be imposed. The same rule applies to a spouse trust which is created under a will. Each child of the deceased gets a deduction of up to $100,000 and a "child-in-law" gets the same amount minus the deduction claimed by his or her spouse. In addition to the $100,000 deduction for children, if a child is under 26 years of age, he or she is entitled to an additional deduction of $2,000 for each year of difference between 26 and his or her age at the time of death, with a $50,000 limit. Thus, if you left $75,000 to your son and $75,000 to your daughter-in-law, your son would be free of tax and your daughter-in-law would have property with a taxable value of $50,000; $75,000 less a deduction of $25,000 (the $100,000 less the $75,000 claimed by her husband). All other beneficiaries get an exemption of $20,000, with grandchildren or great-grandchildren being able to use the unclaimed portion of any allowable deduction of their parents.

Charitable gifts are exempt.

Unlike the Gift Tax Act, the Succession Duty Act imposes tax on a progressive scale. The rates are as follows:

## QUEBEC SUCCESSION DUTY RATES

| Taxable Value | Duty |
|---|---|
| Up to $100,000 | 20% |
| $100,000-$200,000 | $20,000 plus 23% of amount over $100,000 |
| $200,000-$500,000 | $43,000 plus 26% of amount over $200,000 |
| $500,000-$1,000,000 | $121,000 plus 29% of amount over $500,000 |
| $1,000,000-$2,000,000 | $266,000 plus 32% of amount over $1,000,000 |
| Over $2,000,000 | $586,000 plus 35% of amount over $2,000,000 |

It will be noted that an estate can be split up to lower tax. Thus, if father has an estate of $400,000 and leaves a wife and two children, he can leave $100,000 to each child and $200,000 to his widow, free of tax. When mother dies, she can leave each of the children the other $100,000 and again there would be no tax.

There is also a fairly complex series of rules which gives partial relief when the bequest is a farm property or shares in a small business. If you own either of these two types of property, you should consult a tax adviser to help in the planning of the transmission of these assets.

There are a number of special "deeming rules" similar to those in the Gift Tax Act, of which two are the most important. If you have made a gift within three years of death, it is treated as though it is a transmission for succession duty purposes. The amount of the gift will be added in for the purposes of calculating your inheritance, but any gift tax paid will be treated as a credit against succession duties owed.

A second rule will often result in insurance proceeds payable on death being treated as part of the estate. Thus, if your life is insured for $250,000 and your son receives the payment, he is deemed to have received $250,000 from your estate and will be taxable in respect of $150,000. This rule will not apply, however, to the extent that the beneficiary actually paid the insurance premiums. This rule is often side-stepped in the following fashion. Father gifts money to a child with no strings attached, but "suggests" that the insurance premiums be paid. If the payments are made by the child, then any proceeds will be free of succession duties.

Even this brief discussion will indicate that there are serious complexities involved in dealing with the Succession Duty Act. Throughout this chapter, we have stressed that estate planning must be undertaken in conjunction with one or more advisers. Obviously, if you live in Quebec, it is imperative that you get advice from somebody who is familiar with the Succession Duty Act before you undertake something as fundamental as drawing up a will.

**NOTE:**
General publications dealing with wills are available from many insurance and trust companies without charge.

Most large accounting firms also have material for which there is no charge, dealing with various aspects of tax and estate planning. The financial newspapers and magazines in Canada also frequently have articles on this subject. (See "Further Reading" under Drache for additional material.)

# CHAPTER 7

# The Dilemma of Time: Leisure and Retirement

*There is no such thing as "on the way out". As long as you are still doing something interesting and good, you're in business because you're still breathing.*

Louis Armstrong
(1969)

A s you approach retirement, managing your time becomes one of the most important — and sometimes the most diffi- cult — decisions you will have to make. During childhood, your time was structured by your parents and during your working years, much of the day was structured by your job and family responsibilities. Retirement, however, is a stage in life in which you will have a lot more freedom and, therefore, much more unstructured time.

How will you perceive time in retirement? Will you look forward to having free time or will it make you uncomfortable? Will you have so much free time that the days drag? Or so little time that the days seem to fly by? Will you try to "stretch" the day by rising early and retiring late in the evening, or will you try to "shrink" the day by rising late and retiring early? These are important questions that need to be seriously considered before retirement. A person who sees time as something that needs to be "killed" could have a negative attitude towards retirement, resulting in feelings of dissatisfaction. Trying to solve the problem by "keeping busy" with meaningless activities will probably not deliver much enjoyment. In short, a successful retirement depends on your time being used in a meaningful and satisfying way; you must be concerned with the *quality* as well as the *quantity* of the time in retirement.

Leisure was once considered non-productive, less important, and less valuable than time spent working. Today, however, that attitude has changed; leisure is recognized as a necessary part of a contemporary lifestyle and an important source of personal satisfaction and well-being. Thus, while the relative importance of work and leisure may vary at different stages in your life (for instance, work may have a much higher priority for a young adult just establishing a career), at no time should the value of leisure be ignored, or should leisure be regarded as an unacceptable alternative to work. With the great increase in unstructured free time that comes with retirement, it becomes even more important to develop a positive attitude towards leisure.

Learning to manage your time in retirement can be more difficult than learning to manage time at work. Not only will there be a dramatic increase in the amount of free time available, but there will be many more options as to how this time can be used. For example, you could expand the time devoted to pre-retirement leisure activities, re-introduce activities that were pursued earlier in life, or initiate brand new activities. For some people, deciding what to do with all the extra time and making the choices can be real problems. Still, even though the decisions are important, making them should *not* be a source of stress. Ideally, the management of leisure should be seen as a challenge or an opportunity. Most people can look forward to at least ten or fifteen years of healthy leisure following retirement. Think of how much you accomplish between the ages of ten and twenty or between twenty and thirty-five. The same potential for personal accomplishment lies before you in retirement.

Obviously, there is no single correct way to structure time in retirement, no one recipe or prescription for a satisfying and meaningful use of leisure time. Each person is unique, and factors such as health, income, location and type of residence, marital

# LEISURE TIME CLOCK

**Before retirement**

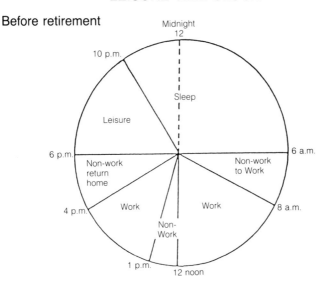

**After Retirement**

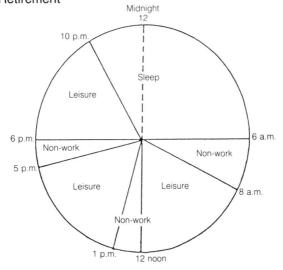

These diagrams are reproduced from *It's Up To You! Planning for leisure and retirement: A handbook for leaders of industrial and business pre-retirement programs* (1979), with the permission of the Ontario Ministry of Tourism and Recreation, Recreation Branch.

status, education, and so on can all affect the retirement experience, and the ways you can and will use your time. However, the sections that follow offer both some general principles and some specific suggestions about leisure. Together they point out the kinds of issues that should be considered when you go about planning for a meaningful use of your leisure in retirement.

## PLANNING FOR LEISURE TIME IN RETIREMENT

In the past, it has been assumed that retirement initiated a gradual process of disengagement. The retiree gave up not only the work role, but also, gradually, the frequency and intensity of involvement in other social and leisure activities. This pattern was influenced by an informal social norm wherein the elderly were encouraged or required to step aside so the young could participate more fully in society. It was also influenced by the myth that declining health and energy were inevitable, and therefore social participation in the post-retirement years should be decreased considerably or avoided entirely.

Today it is considered socially acceptable and desirable for older adults not only to continue to pursue long-standing interests and activities, but also to initiate new activities. Far from disengagement, a pattern of continuous involvement and a search for new interests has become an ideal model for adjusting to retirement.

*Involvement* is the key word. In retirement, just as in any other stage of life, you must be stimulated — physically, mentally, emotionally, and socially — in order to avoid feelings of apathy, disorientation, and social isolation. Studies have shown that retirees who participate in a variety of meaningful activities are more satisfied than those who participate in only one or two activities, or those who do not know how to utilize their time. Still, it is important to emphasize that it is not enough just to keep busy: the quality of the activity is more important than the frequency of the activity or the total number of activities pursued. Activities, whether new or familiar, should be challenging and of sufficient complexity that they are not simply mindless, time-filling pursuits.

If you feel good about what you're doing, you'll probably feel good about yourself. Unlike the other stages in your life, in retirement, *you* are primarily responsible for deciding what you'll do, for determining the way you'll structure your time. While some people may be happiest just taking things as they come, the people who are most likely to express the greatest satisfaction with retirement are those who have developed a concrete and realistic plan for the use of their time.

## THE TRANSITION FROM WORK TO LEISURE

Ideally, retirement and leisure planning should begin in the early years and continue throughout adulthood. In reality, however, most planning begins relatively late, if at all, thereby often preventing a successful transition to a leisure lifestyle. Thus, thinking about leisure alternatives and the meaning of leisure in one's life should be initiated in the middle years. The following principles and ideas may help you in this process:

- Plan early, at least five to ten years before you retire.

- Recognize the importance of leisure. It is no longer considered healthy to be totally consumed by your job or see your identity solely in terms of your job. The well-rounded, successful, and mature individual is one who has a commitment to both work and leisure.

- Consult with your spouse, children, and friends about your short- and long-term plans. Decisions about how to structure your leisure time can be difficult, and those closest to you can provide advice and assistance. Above all, your spouse or companion must be intimately involved in any major decisions you make about your lifestyle in retirement. For example, decisions to work, travel, or move involve major lifestyle issues that must be made in consultation with your spouse or companion if mutual harmony and satisfaction are to be realized.

- Expand your social network. The friendships that are based in the work situation are often difficult to maintain in retirement. If, prior to retirement, you can establish new social contacts, the transition from work to retirement is likely to be that much smoother.

- Consider the obstacles. One of the first steps in developing a realistic plan for the use of leisure time is to recognize the factors that may limit your choice of activities, either immediately or at some time in the future. These might include insufficient financial resources; declining health or energy; lack of transportation (either public or private) for access to events or programs; the unavailability of desired activities in your community; or the loss of interest in an activity after a long period of involvement. An honest appraisal of your present and future situation can help prevent the frustration and disappointment you will feel if you make plans that cannot be realized.

• Do not initiate any drastic changes from your present lifestyle. If you are contemplating a major lifestyle change — such as a move to the south, a move to the country, or a move from a house into an apartment — wherever possible have a "trial run". Thoroughly explore the consequences of any change *before* you make it: Will you miss your garden, your friends and children, the changing seasons?

• Plan for a gradual transition from work to retirement. Since a major goal of retirement planning is to learn how to turn empty free time into meaningful leisure, gradual retirement — wherever possible — is often more successful than sudden withdrawal. In this way, you can discover the effect on your lifestyle of a lessened work role before complete retirement. This can involve working fewer hours per day or week, not taking work home at night or on the weekends, or increasing the length or number of vacations. Alternatively, especially for those who are strongly tied to their jobs, a process of gradual disengagement can occur following the formal retirement date. In this plan, you decrease your work commitment from full time to one-half to one-quarter time to zero over a two- or three-year period. During these periods of reduced work commitment, you should consciously try out the lifestyle or activities that you see as part of your retirement plan (for instance, spending the winter months in the south). In this way, the plan can be tested to determine if it will provide sufficient satisfaction and meaning for you.

## The Importance of Meaningful Leisure

As earlier stated, your goal during retirement is not merely to fill time, but to become involved in activities that are genuinely satisfying. While this will mean something different for each person, the following are some general points that should be considered when planning for the meaningful use of leisure in retirement:

• Retirement activities do not have to be useful or necessary (producing a product, doing volunteer work). It doesn't matter whether others perceive your leisure pursuits as productive or socially desirable. Rather, the meaning and enjoyment *you* derive from an activity should be the important criteria. Evaluate your activities independently, not in comparison with those of others. If an activity (bird-watching, taking a university degree, whatever) provides you with satisfaction, continue that activity even if you are the only person in your social milieu who is engaged in that activity. In short, you should pursue activities that interest you instead of trying to adopt activities you *think* you should be involved in.

• Leisure plans should extend over a number of months or years. Establish priorities concerning activities to be continued or initiated, both short-term (this year and next) and long-term (for the next five to ten years). At the same time, try to maintain flexibility in your interests and social activities in order to take advantage of new opportunities of to deal with changing circumstances.

---

## LEISURE INVENTORY*

a) Things I would like to *stop* doing.
b) Things I enjoy doing *alone.*
c) Things I enjoy doing with *people.*
d) Things I would like to *continue* doing.
e) Things I do *well.*
f) Things I would like to *try.*
g) Things I would like to do *more of* (when I have more time).
h) Things I would like to *learn to do well.*
i) Things I enjoy doing that *cost less than $5.00.*
j) Things I enjoy doing with my *spouse.*
k) Great *experiences I have had* (make you feel good, glad to be alive).
l) Great experiences I *would like to have* (dreams that you wish would come true).
m) Things that require a *risk* (physical, emotional, educational, financial).

---

* This material is reproduced from *It's Up To You! Planning for leisure and retirement: A handbook for leaders of industrial and business pre-retirement programs* (1979), with the permission of the Ontario Ministry of Tourism and Recreation, Recreation Branch.

• Maintain some continuity. Frequently, the leisure pattern established in the middle years influences the way in which time is utilized in retirement. Although continuity is not essential it can be an important factor in making the transition from work to retirement. Look at your long-standing interests and see which you might want to pursue in more depth or in new directions.

• Pursue a number of different types of activities, rather than specializing in one activity in which you may later lose interest. Specifically, you should initiate a variety of activities that provide physical, emotional and intellectual stimulation and satisfaction.

• Exercise your mind and your body. Engage in a hobby, learn a new skill, take an adult education course, seek volunteer work, travel, read. Keep physically active on a regular basis by walking, exercising, hiking, biking, swimming, or playing competitive sports with your peers. Whatever your interests, be an active participant, not merely an observer.

• Retirement is the perfect time to try out new activities to see if they are or might be of interest to you. However, instead of waiting until retirement, test your interest in these new experiences beforehand. Upon completion of the trial run, you'll be in a better position to decide if the new activities are sufficiently rewarding to become part of your retirement plans.

• Ignore supposed sex differences in leisure pursuits; they matter less than you think, especially for seniors. A man who's interested in cooking should take a course in it, as should a woman who might be interested in woodworking or car repairs. Don't just do the things you're "supposed" to do — do the things you *want* to do.

• Be assertive in expressing your needs and interests to community agencies. There are various groups such as Pensioners Concerned, United Pensioners of Ontario, and Advisory Councils in most provinces that are actively involved in speaking up for the rights of older people. Do not passively accept a lack of programs or facilities for older people. If you're not prepared to stand up for you rights, you can't very well expect someone else to do it for you.

## Structuring Your Time in Retirement

Given the great increase in free time that retirement brings, structuring it can seem like a major problem for many people. In addition to the general considerations given above, the following steps could be useful in the process of planning for leisure:

• Summarize the ways you have spent your time at work, at leisure, and with your family. Identify the common recurring themes or activities, and plan to build upon or expand in these areas during retirement, providing they are still enjoyable. With regard to leisure pursuits, it might help to think in terms of categories such as hobbies, arts and crafts, reading, educational, cultural, and physical activity (both competitive and non-competitive), volunteer work, social activities, travel, and job-related pursuits. For each activity you participated in, would like to have done, or would like to do in the future, indicate WHY you wanted to engage in the activity or WHY you wish to pursue it now. Then, evaluate your reasons and either return to those earlier activities, or try other activities that will provide the same type of satisfaction, enjoyment, or meaning.

---

### MY CHART FOR SATISFYING ACTIVITIES*

| | 1 | 2 | 3 |
|---|---|---|---|
| (A) | Activities We Enjoy Together | Satisfactions Received | Possible New Activities |
| (B) | Activities I Enjoy with family, friends | Satisfactions Received | Possible New Activities |
| (C) | Leisure, Recreational Activities I Enjoy | Satisfactions Received | Possible New Activities |

---

* This chart is reproduced from *Options: A handbook of retirement information and exercises for individuals and partners shifting gears and planning their leisure in later years* (1984), with the permission of the Ontario Ministry of Tourism and Recreation, Recreation Branch.

• Keep an activity diary for one week per month for a year, and then evaluate the variety, type, quantity and quality of your leisure at present. The categories given above will help in this process. Have your spouse keep a similar but separate diary, and then compare the two. These diaries can serve as the basis for concrete plans, both individually and as part of a couple.

• You and your spouse should independently respond to, and discuss your responses to, the following questions:
Will earning money still be important and/or necessary?
If so, what skills can be transferred into a profitable enterprise?
How important is it for you to be creative and productive? Is this related to your need to be recognized and known?
Do you prefer to engage in activities alone or with others? If with others, who are these people? Will they be available in retirement?
What did you always want to do with your life during your leisure time? Is this a realistic option for the retirement years?
In physical activity, how important is winning versus having fun when playing games? How can your competitive needs be met in retirement? Should they continue to be a need? What can be substituted for this competitive need if a decline in health status precludes competition?

• Discuss with your spouse possible individual and joint activities. Establish priorities for the activities you intend to either initiate or continue, individually and together.

• In the selection of leisure activities, make sure that you include, as a minimum, at least three activities of which one is primarily *physical,* one *intellectual,* and one *social.*

## LEISURE ACTIVITIES IN RETIREMENT

Do you plan to limit yourself to what are perceived as the traditional, stereotypical activities of the elderly — things like shuffleboard, visiting and television viewing — or do you plan to explore new areas? Leisure involves free choice as to when, where and how your time will be used. Some of the types of leisure pursuits, and the factors that should be considered when making plans to adopt them, follow.

# Work After Retirement

While early or normal retirement provides an opportunity for increased leisure and self-development and for a release from the negative aspects of work, you may wish to continue working beyond your normal retirement date. Clearly defined reasons for remaining employed — such as a need for continued income or mental stimulation — must be established if this lifestyle is to provide you with satisfaction. Moreover, certain decisions must be made: Will the work be full-time or part-time? Will you work for an employer or be self-employed? Will you continue in the same field or start in a new one? The following are some of the things that you should do or consider with regard to working after retirement:

• Identify the most marketable skills you possess.

• Obtain letters of reference prior to retiring from your first career.

• Consider a second career as an artist, consultant or craftsman in which you can change a hobby or interest into a new entrepreneurial endeavour.

• Volunteer to work for a service or business organization, or an individual, that could use your skills and expertise.

# Senior Citizen Centres

Senior Citizen Centres are not everyone's answer for meaningful leisure and social interaction. However, they should be considered and used as a starting point. As well as providing a social milieu, recreational facilities, and formal and informal programs, they also serve as an important source of information.

Centres can be located by consulting the telephone book or a community information office. Visit or call to find out what's available in your area. Typical offerings may include educational programs, games such as pool or cards, arts and crafts supplies, facilities and instruction, income tax advice and assistance, transportation by volunteer drivers, nutritional advice and inexpensive, nutritional meals, health information and medical referrals, meals on wheels for shut-ins, foster grandparent programs, postal security alert, home-help services, and a variety of volunteer services. In short, these centres are not just for "old" people;

rather, they provide a variety of needed services in the community.

## Voluntary Associations and Volunteering

Volunteer work and joining voluntary associations is an important form of leisure at all stages of life. Volunteering not only provides an opportunity for social interaction, but it also offers a way for an individual to continue to contribute to society, as well as acquire status and identity. This type of leisure activity can involve formal organizations, or it can be as informal and unstructured as one neighbour helping another on a regular or infrequent basis.

In order to become a volunteer, you should first make an inventory of your skills, interests, knowledge and expertise. Then, approach individuals, groups, or organizations to see if your skills can be used to serve specific individuals or the community. Some settings for possible volunteer work include libraries, schools, day-care, or senior citizen centres, hospitals, conserva tion groups, community social services or recreational agencies, and small businesses. In these settings you may work with seniors only or people of all ages.

Alternatively, you may have the interests and skills to establish a voluntary organization that is operated by and for your age peers. This organization might be centred in the community at large, in your own neighbourhood, in a nursing home, in a church, or in a senior citizen apartment complex or retirement community. If you are interested in forming such an organization, investigate the federal New Horizons program. Established in 1972 by Health and Welfare Canada to promote the social participation of older adults, New Horizons provides operating grants for projects that are organized and run by seniors themselves. To qualify, projects must be non-profit and of no commercial benefit to others, and could include sports and recreation programs, educational and cultural projects, and social or informational services. In order to apply for a New Horizons grant, a group of at least 10 people, most of whom are older and permanently retired, must agree to serve as voluntary project directors. Grants are given to support projects for an 18-month period, and extensions for an additional period are possible.

Those who have been volunteers earlier in life are more likely to become volunteers in retirement, but people without experience in this type of leisure role can still find volunteering to be the start of a rewarding and challenging second career. Volunteering is an essential component of our economy, and retirees can and should provide — not just receive — services. Without volunteer labour many social services would never be offered or else be prohibitively expensive. Thus, in addition to providing structure and meaning to the life of the retiree, volunteer work is necessary for the economic and social well-being of the community.

## Education in Retirement

Education was once considered to be the exclusive domain of youth, but now learning is seen as both a lifelong necessity and a valuable leisure pursuit. An individual, regardless of age, who has the motivation and opportunity can learn new skills and acquire new knowledge. It is therefore not surprising that enrollment in educational courses is increasing for those over 55.

Courses are available through high schools, community colleges, and universities. They can be offered either on or off campus, and can be either credit or non-credit. At many institutions, tuition fees are either waived or greatly reduced for those over 65, and frequently normal admission requirements are also waived for seniors who wish to enrol in an undergraduate program. To assist older students, many colleges and universities provide counselling programs. Additionally, there are many excellent correspondence programs available from various institutions for those unable to attend regular classes.

Another source of educational programs for older students is Elderhostel, a North American organization that offers one and two week residential programs on various campuses during the summer months. These are "learning vacations" in which an educational program is combined with some leisure and social activities. The Elderhostel programs are reasonably priced and have proved to be quite popular. Information can be obtained by contacting Elderhostel offices listed in the telephone directory, or by enquiring at your local university or college.

## Television Viewing — The Pros and Cons

This is the medium most frequently selected by the elderly for entertainment and information. While not the ideal companion for those who live alone, television may substitute or compensate for a lack of face-to-face interaction with others and serve as "company" to counteract loneliness. Also, television may provide a way of structuring the day, in which the times for meals, chores and sleeping are regulated by the schedule of favourite programs. However, despite these potentially useful functions, it is important that retirees not become overly dependent on television, especially during the early years of retirement. It is an easy way to kill time, but for the most part offers little meaningful social, intellectual, or physical stimulation. Therefore, it might be a good idea to consciously limit the amount of television viewing in order to have the time and opportunity to participate in a variety of other activities.

## Physical Activity in Retirement

Why should you be physically active before and during retirement? Quite simply, you will enjoy life more and have a higher quality of life if you are physically active on a regular basis. You are never too old to take advantage of the fun and benefits of physical activity and, fortunately, more and more seniors are doing just that. In fact, it is no longer medically or socially acceptable for the elderly to be sedentary. Consider the following:

• Adults over the age of 60 can be trained to achieve high levels of fitness and performance by participating in graduated programs of walking, jogging, or swimming, regardless of their degree of physical activity in earlier years.

• Exercise is not the fountain of youth, but it can delay the aging process and enhance the quality of life. Individuals who participate in a regular program of physical activity can improve their level of fitness, regardless of age, and thereby improve their stamina and mobility. This in turn can improve efficiency and safety in the performance of daily household tasks.

• An improvement in physical fitness not only increases the likelihood of good health, but it can lead to a longer period of independence, as well as a faster and more complete recovery from some illnesses.

• Participation in a regular program of physical activity may relieve anxiety and fear, increase self-confidence, reduce tension, relieve depression, and improve one's general mood and sense of well-being.

# Getting Fit

*Now* is the time to begin a program of physical activity, but before you start, you should consider the following points:

• Discuss your personal concerns about physical activity with your family physician. Determine to what extent you can participate in physical activities that are more demanding than walking or climbing stairs.

• Consult a physical activities specialist concerning the type of program and activity that is appropriate for you. A specialist of this kind may be available at the local Y, Seniors Centre, or community recreation department.

• To avoid undue stress, learn to monitor your response to physical activity by frequently checking your pulse rate. Your physician or an activity specialist can indicate the maximum heart rate you should have during physical activity.

• Each time you begin any form of physical activity, including household chores like shovelling snow, you should include a 15 minute warm-up period, and a 15 minute cool-down period to allow the circulatory system to return to the normal level.

• Occasionally, regardless of the type of activity, stop, relax, and take a few deep breaths. Do not rush through the activity. Enjoy physical activity, and do not think of it as "bad-tasting" medicine.

• It is normal for people of all ages to feel stiff and to have some sore muscles after beginning an activity program. By being active three times a week, this soreness should disappear in a few weeks.

# Staying Fit

The amount and frequency of physical activity in your daily routine can be increased gradually and progressively even without a formal exercise program. The following are some ways in which you can increase your basic level of physical activity as you engage in your normal daily activities:

• Instead of driving, walk as much as possible.

• Climb stairs instead of using an elevator. Start with one or two flights, then gradually increase the number of flights you climb each week.

• Get on and off a bus one or two stops farther from your home each day. This will increase the amount of daily walking.

• Each day, park your car at an increasingly greater distance from your destination.

• Swim increasingly greater distances two or three times a week. This is an especially good activity for those with knee or hip problems.

• Perform daily stretching exercises to keep your joints flexible. In this way, you will increase the range of motion of each joint. Similarly, you can include bending and stretching in normal household tasks in order to improve flexibility.

• If you find you are sitting or lying for more than an hour, get up and walk around the house for about five minutes. This is also a good time to do some stretching exercises.

The decision to be active or sedentary is yours, but a rocking chair kind of lifestyle is neither healthy nor particularly rewarding. As they say — Use it or lose it!

# APPENDIX   A

# Suggestions for Organizing Retirement Planning Courses

For those individuals who wish to use this book as a resource book in the organization of retirement planning courses, the following material offers some general guidelines.

The one-time retirement planning interview which usually deals only with financial benefits is often inadequate when it is the only information available to the individual. Most people need help in covering the whole range of issues dealt with in this book. However, the opportunity for an individual interview with the benefits officer of an organization is a necessary and helpful adjunct to participation in a seminar series as described here.

## COMPOSITION OF THE GROUP

It generally makes for more effective group interaction if the group comes from much the same educational and socio-economic backgrounds. This does not mean that the seminar has to be rigidly exclusive but, nevertheless, individuals from vastly different socio-economic backgrounds, educational levels and work environments will usually have such different problems and needs that group interaction will be difficult.

Because the most effective courses allow for considerable discussion and interaction, the size of the group should be relatively small. The optimum group size would be from 15 to 20 people but groups of 30 to 35 are certainly manageable.

Where married individuals are involved it is important to invite their spouses to attend. Surveys show that, in the past, women frequently did not know what their financial situation would be during retirement or what questions to ask in relation to this. The attendance of spouses is a useful way to facilitate the discussion of potentially delicate aspects of planning. The group situation offers the opportunity for frank discussions to take place in a calm and objective atmosphere.

## FREQUENCY AND DURATION OF SEMINARS

The frequency or the time frame in which the course takes place will vary according to the circumstances and feasibility for the individuals participating. However, there is a great advantage in the courses being spread over a period of time.

Past experiences have shown that eight sessions over eight consecutive weeks, with each session lasting about two hours, work very well. This format has the advantage of allowing the participants to integrate the material and come back to future sessions with questions and reactions that may not surface immediately. This is difficult to achieve in short condensed programs lasting a day, a day and a half, or two or even three days. Furthermore, the condensed intensive programs often overload information on the participants without leaving proper time for discussion. It is also frequently difficult to release employees from the work situation for one to three days. However, when sessions are given by other than the employers, some compromises may have to be made.

One of the great benefits of the seminar seems to be the kind of group identity and group interaction that develops which is very supportive. It helps the participants to cope with many of the concerns, fears and mixed feelings individuals have when facing retirement or retirement planning.

## GROUP LEADER

It is important to have a knowledgeable and interested group leader for all sessions, and there should be some continuity so that questions can be asked and sessions linked. A group leader or chairperson is the individual who moderates each session and who is knowledgeable in the general area. If a retired individual can be found to act as chairperson there is a great advantage in that he or she also serves as a role model and lends credibility to the concepts. The individual sessions are usually successful if each session is led by an expert in his/her particular field since no one person can really have an in-depth knowledge in the many aspects related to successful retirement planning.

## CORPORATE AND INSTITUTIONAL PROGRAMS

For corporate and institutional programs it is important that a benefits officer be available for one session on financial planning to deal with the particular pension plan or situation of the individuals. If the participants are from different institutions, then of course, general financial planning sessions are still appropriate and the individuals will have to be referred to their own situations for any specific questions about their own particular plans. It is also important that individuals be referred to resources that they can investigate on their own, after being given the necessary information such as reading lists, lists of organizations that might be relevant or other aids for their own perusal.

It has been evident in planning and delivering retirement planning seminars that a resource book as well as recommended readings are most important and helpful. This volume was prepared and written to fill this need. Also included as an appendix is a listing of contact offices in the Territories and Provinces to which individuals can write or telephone for services available to individuals over 65 years of age.

---

# APPENDIX    B

# Community Services for the Retired

As you have discovered by now, planning for retirement is not simply a matter of wistful armchair fantasizing. The pitfalls of a dilettantish approach to planning are dangerous. As Fred Astaire put it: "Old age is like everything else. To make a success of it, you've got to start young." What this book has been stressing is foresight. Therefore, the community services and resources outlined in this chapter should be familiar to you before you retire so that you may cogently evaluate your retirement needs in advance.

## INFORMATION AND REFERRAL SERVICES

To use community services, you first have to know they exist, and that's why we have such things as information and referral services. There are different types of these, but they all have one purpose: to give information, usually over the telephone, about community and government resources available in matters such as housing, health care, education, and leisure activities. They keep up-to-date files and can tell you what services are available in your community. Sometimes they act as the intermediary between a person seeking service and the organization likely to furnish this service. Sometimes they even contact the organization themselves to facilitate and accelerate the procedure.

The most sophisticated referral services will do a follow-up to determine whether the user obtained satisfaction. In this way they are able to determine whether there are any shortcomings or duplication in the services offered.

The federal, provincial and municipal governments have their own referral services. There are also non-government ones and certain volunteer centres which give out information on the resources and services offered in your community.

The contact list that follows lists the major Canadian information and referral services for retirees by province. This list can be found in *The Directory*, a publication of Canadian Pensioners Concerned (see "Further Reading" under Appendix B for complete information).

# CONTACT LIST

## ALBERTA

Senior Citizens Bureau
Senior Citizens Advisory Council

Department of Social Services and Community Health
Seventh Street Plaza
10030 107th Street
Edmonton, Alberta
T5J 3E4

Department of Housing and Public Works
10050 112th Street
Edmonton, Alberta
T5K 1L9

Department of Hospitals and Medical Care
Hys Centre
11010 101st Street
Edmonton, Alberta
T5H 4B9

## BRITISH COLUMBIA

Ministry of Human Resources
Parliament Buildings
Victoria, British Columbia
V8V 1X4

Ministry of Lands, Parks and Housing
Housing Programs Branch
838 Fort Street
Victoria, British Columbia
V8V 2V7

Ministry of Health
Parliament Buildings
Victoria, British Columbia
V8V 2V7

## MANITOBA

Manitoba Council on Aging
238 Portage Avenue
Winnipeg, Manitoba
R3C 0B1

Manitoba Housing and Renewal Corporation
287 Broadway Avenue
Winnipeg, Manitoba
R3C 0R9

Services to Seniors
Manitoba Department of Community Services and Corrections
831 Portage Avenue
Winnipeg, Manitoba
R3G 0N6

Manitoba Department of Health
Legislative Buildings
Winnipeg, Manitoba
R3C 0V8

## NEW BRUNSWICK

Department of Health
Centennial Building
Fredericton, New Brunswick
E3B 5H1

Department of Social Services
Box 6000
Fredericton, New Brunswick
E3B 5H1

New Brunswick Housing Corporation
Box 611
Fredericton, New Brunswick
E3B 5B2

## NEWFOUNDLAND AND LABRADOR

Department of Health
Confederation Building
St. John's, Newfoundland
A1C 5T7

Department of Social Services
Confederation Building
P. O. Box 4750
St. John's, Newfoundland
A1C 5J2

Newfoundland and Labrador Housing Corporation
P. O. Box 220
Elizabeth Towers
St. John's, Newfoundland
A1C 5J2

## NORTHWEST TERRITORIES

Northwest Territories Housing Corporation
P. O. Box 2100
Yellowknife, N.W.T.
X1A 2P6

Department of Social Services
Services to the Aged and Handicapped
Yellowknife, N.W.T.
X1A 2L9

---

## NOVA SCOTIA

Senior Citizens Secretariat
Dennis Building, 6th Floor
P. O. Box 2065
Halifax, Nova Scotia
B3J 2Z1

Department of Social Services
Johnston Building
P. O. Box 696
Halifax, Nova Scotia
B3J 2T7

Nova Scotia Housing Commission
P. O. Box 185
Dartmouth,. Nova Scotia
B2Y 3Z3

Department of Health
Joseph Howe Building
P. O. Box 488
Halifax, Nova Scotia
B3J 2R8

---

## ONTARIO

Ministry of Community and Social Services
6th Floor
Hepburn Block
80 Grosvenor Street
Toronto, Ontario
M7A 1E9

Ministry of Health
Hepburn Block
80 Grosvenor Street
Toronto, Ontario
M7A 1R3

Ontario Advisory Council on Senior Citizens
700 Bay Street
Toronto, Ontario
M5G 1Z6

Income Security Programs — Health and Welfare Canada
789 Don Mills Road
Don Mills, Ontario
M3C 1T5

Ministry of Community and Social Services
110 Eglinton Avenue West, 3rd Floor
Toronto, Ontario
M4R 2C9

Seniors Secretariat
700 Bay St., 3rd Floor
Toronto, Ontario
M5G 1Z6

---

## PRINCE EDWARD ISLAND

Department of Health and Social Services
Health Branch
Sullivan Building
Box 3000
Charlottetown, P.E.I.
C1A 7P1

Department of Health and Social Services
Social Services Branch
Sullivan Building
P. O. Box 3000
Charlottetown, P.E.I.
C1A 7N8

Prince Edward Island Housing Corporation
11 Kent Street
P. O. Box 1388
Charlottetown, P.E.I.
C1A 7N1

---

## QUÉBEC

Ministère des Affaires Sociales
Service des Politiques aux Adultes et aux Personnes Âgées
1005 Chemin Ste. Foy
Québec, P. Q.
G1S 4N4

Société d'Habitation du Québec
1054 Rue Conroy, 4e étage
Building G, Block 3
Québec, P. Q.
G1R 5E7

Régie de l'Assurance-Maladie du Québec
P. O. Box 6600
Québec, P. Q.
G1K 7T3

---

## SASKATCHEWAN

Saskatchewan Department of Health
T. C. Douglas Building
3475 Albert Street
Regina, Saskatchewan
S4S 6X6

Saskatchewan Housing Corporation
800 Chetemere Plaza
2500 Victoria Avenue
Regina, Saskatchewan
S4P 3V7

Saskatchewan Department of Social Services
1920 Broad Street
Regina, Saskatchewan
S4P 3V6

Senior Citizens Provincial Council
Room 540
Avord Tower
2002 Victoria Avenue
Regina, Saskatchewan
S4P 3V7

## YUKON

Department of Health and Human Resources
Box 2703
Whitehorse, Yukon Territory
Y1A 2C6

# HOUSING AND RELATED PROGRAMS FOR SENIOR CITIZENS

Before you retire, it's important that you think about the kind of life you want to lead and take stock of your preferences, aspirations, habits, and, especially, your means. Obviously the choice of a new location or type of dwelling must be based on its affordability and the fact that it reflects the lifestyle you want for yourself.

For those who need help with housing, there are a number of programs available at the federal, provincial and municipal levels:

## Federal Programs

**Residential Rehabilitation Assistance Program:**
Funds are made available from the Canada Mortgage and Housing Corporation to assist in the improvement of sub-standard dwellings.

**Non-Profit Co-operatives:**
Federal funding for start-up costs are made available to a non-profit co-operative.

**Private Non-Profit Co-operatives:**
The National Housing Act offers various forms of assistance to privately owned, non-profit, low-income rental housing, usually in the form of an insured mortgage.

**Home Improvement Loans:**
The National Housing Act provides chartered banks and approved installment credit agencies with authority to make loans and home improvement, and the Canada Mortgage and Housing Corporation guarantees these loans.

## Provincial Programs

**Alberta:**
Senior Citizens Self-Contained Housing Program
One-Third Capital Grant Program
Alberta Pioneer Repair Program
Home Adaptation Program
Renters Assistance Grants
Property Tax Rebate
Renters Assistance for Mobile-Home Owners

**British Columbia:**
Senior Citizen Housing Construction Program
B. C. Shelter Aid for Elderly Renters
Home Conversion Loan Program
Deferment of Property Taxes
Renters Tax Credit

**Manitoba:**
Elderly Persons Housing Program
Shelter Allowance for Elderly Renters
Critical Home Repair Program
Property Tax Credit
Pensioner Tenants School Tax Assistance Program

**New Brunswick:**
Public Housing for Senior Citizens
Rental Assistance to the Elderly
Home Improvement Loans

**Newfoundland and Labrador:**
Public Housing Programs
Rent Supplement Program

**Northwest Territories:**
Public Housing Program
Senior Citizens Accommodation
Social Housing Program

**Nova Scotia:**
Public Housing Program
Rental Assistance Program for Senior Citizens
Senior Citizens Assistance Program

Provincial Housing Emergency Repair Program
Small Loans Assistance Program
Property Tax Rebate

**Ontario:**
Ontario Home Renewal Program
Senior Citizens Assisted Housing
Rent Supplement Program
Ontario Property Tax Grants

**Prince Edward Island:**
Senior Citizens Housing Program
The Essential Home Repair Program
Provincial Contribution to Seniors
The Rural Residential Rehabilitation Assistance Program

**Quebec:**
Logirente (Rent Supplement)
Logipop (Co-op)
Laginone (Home Renovation)
Logelm (Public Housing)

**Saskatchewan:**
Public Housing for Senior Citizens
Senior Citizens Home Repair Program
Residential Rehabilitation Assistant Program
Non-Profit Housing for Senior Citizens
Home Modification for the Physically Disabled
Renters Property Tax Rebate Program
Mortgage Rebate
School Tax Rebate

**Yukon:**
Pioneer Utility Grant

For further information on any of these programs, please contact the
information and referral services listed above.

# HEALTH CARE AND SOCIAL SERVICES FOR SENIOR CITIZENS

## In the Home

Not so long ago, old people who couldn't take care of themselves and
had no one else to take care of them had no choice but to live in old-
age homes. Today, a wide range of community and social services are
available to ensure that the elderly receive whatever assistance they
require for as long as necessary. Healthcare and home-care services are
available for the elderly on a temporary or long-term basis in the home.
Similarly, home maintenance services and meal delivery services are
provided in many communities. For those who feel isolated, accom-
paniment services and friendship visits can be arranged.

## At Day-Care And Senior Citizen Centres

Some of the services offered in the home are also available in various centres if the recipient is sufficiently mobile to get to one. Day-care centres have been established in most communities to provide social services for seniors who are still living at home but who need some form of assistance to retain or increase their current level of autonomy. In some instances, facilities exist for admitting seniors on a regular or temporary basis, where required.

Senior Citizen Centres offer a wide range of recreational and educational activities as well as specific problem-solving services to seniors. Run by the members themselves, these centres differ from day-care centres in that they offer a wider range of activities but few medical or care services.

## Provincial Programs

**Alberta:**
Adult Day-Care
Community Health Nursing Service
Alberta Co-ordinated Homecare Program
Family and Community Support Services Programs
Transportation for the Elderly and Handicapped

**British Columbia:**
Adult Day-Care Centres
Public Health Nursing Services
Homecare — Long-Term Care Program
Community Projects Funding Program
Community Nutritionist Program
Seniors Day Centres
Bus Passes
Bus Courtesy Fares for Senior Citizens
Homemakers Services Program — Long-Term Care Program

**Manitoba:**
Adult Day Care
Seniors Centres
Home Care
Provincial Public Health Nursing Services

**New Brunswick:**
Community-Based Services to Seniors
Home Care
Seniors Day-Care Programs
Extra Mural Hospital

**Newfoundland and Labrador:**
Visiting Home Nursing Service
Home Care Programs

**Northwest Territories:**
Co-ordinated Home Care

**Nova Scotia:**
Home Care
Homemakers Services
Community Health Units

**Ontario:**
Visiting Homemakers and Nurses Services Program
Elderly Persons Centres
Health Units
Acute Home-Care Program
Chronic Home-Care Program
Home Support Program for the Elderly

**Prince Edward Island:**
Day-Care Programs
Homecare
Visiting Homemakers Services

**Quebec:**
Home Care Program
Day Centres

**Saskatchewan:**
Senior Care Centres
Saskatchewan Home Care Program
Transportation Services for the Aged
Transportation Services for the Handicapped

**Yukon**
Handy Bus

For further information on any of these programs, please contact the information and referral services listed above.

# EDUCATIONAL PROGRAMS FOR SENIOR CITIZENS

There are two general types of educational services widely available to senior citizens. The first is courses in pre-retirement planning offered by various organizations, including employers, unions, government departments, and private counsellors. The course material varies widely and is usually tailored to the specific needs of the participants.

The second broad type of educational service is in the area of continuing education. Courses are available at the full range of levels and most Canadian universities offer seniors the opportunity to enroll in undergraduate courses free of charge.

For information on educational services available in your community, please contact the information and referral services listed above.

# CULTURAL AND RECREATIONAL PROGRAMS FOR SENIOR CITIZENS

## Federal Programs

Life offers many opportunities for serving others, especially when you remember that the quality of a community depends on the quality of the relationships between individuals within it. "New Horizons" is a federal program designed to encourage retired persons to take up activities that serve the community. Established in 1972 by Health and Welfare Canada, this program provides operating grants for projects that are organized and run by seniors. To qualify, projects must be non-profit and of no commercial benefit to others, and a group of at least ten persons, the majority of whom are older and permanently retired, must agree to serve as voluntary project directors. The range of projects which are granted funds is vast and many include sports, recreation, and crafts programs; historical, educational and cultural projects; information services; and activity centres.

## Provincial Programs

**British Columbia:**
Community Involvement Program
Free Camping Privileges
Hunting and Fishing Licences

**Manitoba:**
An Outreach Program
Seniors' Olympics

**Ontario:**
Ontario Senior Citizens' Privilege Card
Grants for Community Facilities
Field Services
Wintario

**Quebec:**
Holiday Camps
The Discovering Quebec Program
A Subsidy Program for Special Institutions
The Federation of Golden Age Clubs

**Saskatchewan:**
Saskatour
Senior Activity Centres
Recreation for the Handicapped Grants

For further information on any of these programs, please contact the information and referral services listed above.

# OTHER PROGRAMS FOR SENIOR CITIZENS
## Physical Activities

Fitness will be as important to you when you are retired as it is now. Many physical-health organizations have set up keep-fit programs for the elderly. Government efforts include Participaction and the Manitoba Seniors' Olympics, among many others. The private sector runs numerous fitness clubs that have special programs for seniors. For information on physical activities for seniors available in your community, please contact the information and referral services listed earlier under Provincial Programs.

## Travel Services

Travel is said to be broadening for the young, but in reality it is a good education at any age. If you have ever dreamed of exploring a mysterious or intriguing part of the world, retirement provides you with the time to realize that dream. Travel bureaus geared to the needs of seniors exist in many communities. Many national parks offer services and special group services for seniors. An international corporation called Elderhostel Inc. offers educational programs where groups of seniors board at a university or college in Canada, the United States, or overseas, and can take courses and participate in socio-cultural visits. Current editions of the Elderhostel catalogue are available at public libraries across Canada. You can also receive a free copy by writing to: Elderhostel Canada, University of New Brunswick, P.O. Box 4400, Fredericton, N.B. E3B 5A3.

For information on travel services for seniors available in your community, please contact the information and referral services listed earlier under Provincial Programs.

## Legal Aid Services

Legal aid is guaranteed by law and is subsidized by federal-provincial cost-sharing arrangements. Legal assistance is provided for anyone who does not have the financial resources to exercise a right, obtain legal counsel, or enlist the services of a lawyer or notary. As an older citizen, you may require a broad range of legal services: protection of your rights as a consumer or tenant, financial planning, estate planning, or victim compensation. To obtain information on legal aid services available in your community, please contact the information and referral services listed earlier under Provincial Programs.

# CONCLUSION

While the services described above are primarily geared to the elderly retired person, it is your responsibility to be aware of them now, before they become essential. In planning your retirement, community services are an integral part of the equation you should use to calculate your future.

# FURTHER READING

### 1. Planning for Change: Psychological Aspects of Retirement

"HOW TO" GUIDES

Allen, R.T. *Today is the Frist Day of the Rest of Your Life.* Toronto: McClelland & Stewart, 1971.

Bradford, Leland P., and M.I. Bradford. *Retirement: Coping with Emotional Upheavals.* Chicago: Nelson Hall Publishers, 1979.

Canada. Department of Labour. *Pre-Retirement Planning.* Ottawa, 1975.

Dangott, Lillian R., and R.A. Kalish. *A Time to Enjoy: The Pleasures of Aging.* New Jersey: Prentice-Hall, 1979.

Dickinson, Peter A. *The Complete Retirement Planning Book: Your Guide to Happiness, Health and Financial Success.* New York: E.P. Dutton, 1976.

Foner, A., and K. Schwab. *Aging and Retirement.* Monterey, CA: Brooks/Cole Publishing Company, 1981.

Hunnisett, Henry S. *Retirement Guide for Canadians: Plan Now for a Comfortable Future.* Vancouver, B.C.: International Self-Counsel Press Ltd., 1983.

Lazarus, Morden. *Looking Forward: A Guide for Retirement.* Toronto: CPA Publishers, 1983. Available from: Canadian Council of Retirees, 15 Gervais Dr., Don Mills, Ontario M3C 1Y8.

McLeish, John A.B. *The Challenge of Aging: Ulyssean Paths to Creative Living.* Vancouver, B.C.: Douglas & McIntyre, 1983.

Watt, Jill, and Ann Calder. *I Love You But You Drive Me Crazy: A Guide for Caring Relatives.* Second edition, revised. Vancouver, B.C.: F. Forbez, 1982.

Weinstein, Grace W. *Life Plans: Looking Forward to Retirement.* New York: Holt, Rinehart & Winston, 1979.

SOCIOLOGICAL/HISTORICAL

Auerbach, Lewis, and A. Gerber. *Implications of the Changing Age Structure of the Canadian Population.* Ottawa: Science Council of Canada, 1976.

Baum, Daniel J. *The Final Plateau: The Betrayal of Our Older Citizens.* Toronto: Burns & MacEachern, 1974.

Butler, R.N., and M.I. Lewis. *Aging and Mental Health: Positive Psychosocial and Biomedical Approaches.* Third edition. St. Louis: C.V. Mosby, 1982.

de Beauvoir, Simone. *Old Age.* Trans. Patrick O'Brian. London: Deutsch, Weindenfeld and Nicolson, 1972.

McAvoy, Leo H. "Needs of the Elderly: An Overview of the Research". *Parks and Recreation* (March 1977): 31-35.

Shanas, Ethel, ed. *Aging in Contemporary Society.* Beverley Hills, CA: Sage Publications, 1970.

## 2. New Tricks: Lifestyle in Retirement

Atchley, R.C. *The Social Forces in Later Life: An Introduction to Social Gerontology.* Second edition. Belmont, CA: Wadsworth Publishing, 1977.

Hills, L. Rust. *How to Retire at Forty-One: Or Dropping Out of the Rat Race Without Going Down the Drain.* Garden City, N.Y.: Doubleday, 1973.

Hunnisset, Henry S. *How to Survive Retirement in Canada.* North Vancouver, B.C.: International Self-Counsel Press Ltd., 1975.

Morris, Peter. *Loss and Change.* Garden City, N.Y.: Anchor Press, Doubleday, 1975.

Phipps, Joyce. *Death's Single Privacy: Growing and Personal Growth.* New York: Seabury, 1974.

Rogers, Elizabeth. *For Widows Only.* Victoria, B.C.: The Widows Information Centre, 620 View St., 1976.

Vickery, Florence. "The Use of Time and Social Adjustments in the Retirement Years". *Creative Programming for Older Adults.* New York: Association Press, 1974.

## 3. Roosting and the Empty Nest: Living Arrangements in Retirement

### BOOKS

Chellis, R.D., J.F. Seagle Jr., and B.M. Seagle, eds. *Congregate Housing for Older People: A Solution for the 1980s.* Lexington, MA: Lexington Books, D.C. Heath, 1982.

Dickinson, Peter A. *Sunbelt Retirement: The Complete State-by-State Guide to Retiring in the South and West of the United States.* Second edition. New York: E.P. Dutton, 1980.

Gunn, Jonathan, J. Verkley, and L. Newman. *Older Canadian Homeowners: A Literature Review.* Ottawa: CMHC, 1983.

Kushner, Carol, P.L. Falta, and A. Aitkens. *Making Your Home Accessible: A Disabled Consumer's Guide.* Ottawa: Ministry of Consumer & Corporate Affairs, 1983.

### ARTICLES

Beland, F. "The Decision of Elderly Persons to Leave Their Homes". *Gerontologist,* 24(April 1984):179-185.

Fengler, A.P., N. Danigelish, and V.C. Little. "Later Life Satisfaction and Household Structure: Living with Others and Living Alone". *Aging and Society,* 3(November 1983):357-377.

Fletcher, Susan, and L.O. Stone. "The Living Arrangements of Older Women". *Essence,* 4(1980):115-133.

Hare, P.H., and M. Haske. "Innovative Living Arrangements: A Source of Long Term Care". *Aging,* 342(December/January, 1983-84): 3-8.

Harkey, P.W., and H.G. Traxler. "Share a Home: A Unique Community-based Residential Alternative for the Dependent Elderly". *Journal of Applied Gerontology,* 1(1982):90-94.

Mayer, N.S., and Olson Lee. "Federal Home Repair Programs and Elderly Homeowners' Needs". *Gerontologist,* 21 (June 1981):312-322.

Mindel, Charles, H. "Multigenerational Family Households: Recent Trends and Implications for the Future". *Gerontologist,* 15(April 1975):160-164.

Murphy, Peter E. "Condominiums and the Elderly: A Convenient Marriage or a Marriage of Convenience?" *Habitat,* 18(1975).

Nelson, L.M., and M. Winter. "Life Disruption, Independence, Satisfaction, and the Consideration of Moving". *Gerontologist,* 15(April 1975): 160-164.

Ypes, M. "The Retirement Community". *Ontario Nursing Homes,* 13(June/ July 1982): 4-5.

## 4. Frankly, Doctor...: Your Health During Retirement

Butler, R.N., and M.I. Lewis. *Sex after Sixty: A Guide for Men and Women for Their Later Years.* New York: Harper & Row, 1976.

*Don't Take It Easy: Fitness for the Older Canadian.* Ottawa: Ministry of Fitness and Amateur Sport, 1981. (Fitness and Amateur Sport, 365 Laurier Avenue West, Ottawa, Ontario K1A 0X6).

Gordon, Michael. *An Ounce of Prevention: The Canadian Guide to a Healthy and Successful Retirement.* Scarborough, Ontario: Prentice-Hall Canada Inc., 1984.

Gordon, Michael. *Old Enough to Feel Better: A Medical Guide for Seniors.* Toronto: Key Porter, 1981.

Knopf, O. *Successful Aging.* Boston: G.K. Hall & Co., 1977.

leRiche, W.H. *The Complete Family Book of Nutrition and Meal Planning.* Toronto: Methuen, 1980.

## 5. Taking It With You: Financial Planning for Retirement

Bartel, H., and M. Daly. "Reverse Annuity Mortgages as a Source of Retirement Income". *Canadian Public Policy,* 6(1980): 584-590.

Canada. Health and Welfare. Public Affairs Directorate. *Better Pensions for Canadians.* Ottawa, 1982.

Canada. House of Commons. Clerk of the Special Committee on Pension Reform. Committees and Private Legislation Branch. *Report of the Parliamentary Task Force on Pension Reform.* Ottawa, 1983.

Canadian Labour Congress. Education Department. *The Pension Story.* Ottawa, 1980.

Drache, Arthur B.C., ed. *The Canada Estate Planning Service.* Toronto: Richard De Boo Ltd., 1980.

Drache, Arthur B.C. *It's Your Future: The Canadian Guide to Estate Planning.* Toronto: McClelland & Stewart, 1984.

Economic Council of Canada. *One in Three—Pensions for Canadians to 2030,* 1979.

Grenby, Mike. *Mike Grenby's Tax Tips: How to Pay Less Tax This Year.* Vancouver, B.C.: International Self-Counsel Press, 1984.

Haley, D. *Report of the Royal Commission on the Status of Pensions in Ontario,* 1981.

Lazar, Harvey. *The Retirement Income System in Canada: Problems and Alternatives.* Report of the Task Force on Retirement Income Policy, 1979.

## 6. Leaving It Behind: Estate Planning

Drache, Arthur B.C., ed. *The Canada Estate Planning Service.* Toronto: Richard De Boo Ltd., 1980.

Drache, Arthur B.C. *It's Your Future: The Canadian Guide to Estate Planning.* Toronto: McClelland & Stewart, 1984.

## 7. The Dilemma of Time: Leisure and Retirement

Heywood, L. *Recreation for Older Adults: A Program Manual.* Toronto: Ministry of Culture and Recreation, 1979.

Kaplan, M. *Lifestyle and Lifespan.* Toronto: W.B. Saunders, 1979.

Kleiber, D., and J. Kelly. "Leisure, socialization and the life-cycle". In S. Iso-Ahole, ed. *Social Psychological Perspectives on Leisure and Recreation* (91-137). Springfield: Charles C. Thomas, 1980.

McPherson, B.D. "Aging and leisure involvement". In B.D. McPherson. *Aging as a Social Process* (407-435). Toronto: Butterworths, 1983.

McPherson, B.D. *Physical Activity for the Elderly: A Manual for Program Leaders.* Toronto: Ministry of Tourism and Recreation, Recreation Branch, 1984.

Ontario. Ministry of Tourism and Recreation. Recreation Branch. *Physical Activity and the Older Adult: Experience the Challenge and Benefits of Being Active and Fit.* Toronto, 1984.

Osgood, N. *Life After Work: Retirement: Leisure, Recreation and the Elderly.* New York: Praeger Press, 1982.

Sissons, Annabel. *Options: A Handbook of Retirement Information and Exercises for Individuals and Partners Shifting Gears and Planning Their Leisure in Later Years.* Toronto: Ministry of Tourism and Recreation, Recreation Branch, 1984.

Sissons, Annabel, and D. Vigoda. *Leisure Can Be Pleasure: Changing Roles in Retirement.* Toronto: Ministry of Culture and Recreation, 1981.

Sissons, Annabel, and Marion Voege. *It's Up To You! Planning for Leisure and Retirement: A Handbook for Leaders of Industrial and Business Preretirement Programs.* Toronto: Ministry of Tourism and Recreation, Special Services Branch, 1979.

Teague, M. "Aging and Leisure: A Social Psychological Perspective". In S. Iso-Ahola, ed. *Social Psychological Perspectives on Leisure and Recreation* (219-257). Springfield: Charles C. Thomas, 1980.

## Appendix B: Community Services for the Retired

Lang, Cathy, and Carol Shelton. *The Directory: Programs for Senior Citizens Across Canada.* Toronto: Canadian Pensioners Concerned, 1982. (Canadian Pensioners Concerned, Ontario Division, 51 Bond Street, Toronto, Ontario M5B 1X1, 416-368-5222).

*The Directory* lists all programs available for retirees, as well as the addresses of important organizations and government offices serving senior citizens. Compiled in 1983, it is now available from the above address for only $2.

# LIST OF CONTRIBUTORS

*Planning Your Retirement* draws on the expertise of the following academics and professionals from across Canada:

## GENERAL EDITOR AND CONTRIBUTOR

**BLOSSOM T. WIGDOR, Ph.D.**, noted psychologist and gerontologist, is the founding Director of the Programme in Gerontology and Professor of Psychology at the University of Toronto. She is a former Vice-President of the Canadian Association in Gerontology and was a member of the Science Council of Canada from 1973-1979. She is a Fellow of the Canadian Psychological Association and the Gerontological Society of America. The editor-in-chief of the *Canadian Journal on Aging,* she has edited several volumes in gerontology and authored many scientific articles. She has been involved in research and teaching about aging for many years and has developed and delivered numerous pre-retirement seminars.

## CONTRIBUTORS AND CONSULTANTS

**ARTHUR B.C. DRACHE, Q.C.**, is currently a partner in the Ottawa law firm of Drache, Rotenberg & Horwitz. Chief of the Department of Finance's Personal Income Tax Section from 1972-1976, he now teaches part time at Queen's University in Kingston. Winner of the 1977 National Business Writing Award, he is a contributing editor and writer for *The Financial Post,* and has authored, co-authored, or contributed to ten books on taxation and estate planning.

**RORY H.G. FISHER, M.D.**, is Head of the Department of Extended Care, Sunnybrook Medical Centre, Co-ordinator of Geriatric Medicine, and Professor, Department of Family and Community Medicine and Department of Medicine, University of Toronto. He is also a Fellow of McLaughlin College, York Univeristy. He was educated in Dublin and Edinburgh and held a number of medical posts in England. He is the author of a number of scientific articles on health care of the elderly.

**NORAH KEATING, Ph.D.**, is an associate professor in the Departments of Family Studies and Geriatric Medicine at the University of Alberta. She is president of the Alberta Association on Gerontology, on the Board of Directors of the University of Alberta Centre for Gerontology, and an editor of *Foresight Magazine,* a journal for pre-retirement planning.

**BARRY D. McPHERSON, Ph.D.**, is a professor and Graduate Adviser for the Program in Gerontology at the University of Waterloo. Author of the best-seller, *Aging As A Social Process,* he is currently the consulting editor for a forthcoming series of monographs on Individual and Population Aging. His most recent research is related to retirement, leisure, and the quality of life in later years.

**ALBERT ROSE,** Ph.D., is Professor Emeritus and former Dean of the Faculty of Social Work, University of Toronto. He was also a founding member of both the Centre for Urban and Community Studies and the Programme in Gerontology at the University of Toronto. He is presently chairman of the Metropolitan Toronto Housing Authority. He has published five books and numerous articles on the subjects of housing and urban development, and social welfare policy.

**HOWARD S. SEIDEN,** M.D., is Director of the Front-Frederick Health Services in Toronto. He is on active staff at St. Michael's Hospital and is an assistant professor in the Department of Family and Community Medicine at the University of Toronto. Well known for his media profile and medical writings, his syndicated medical column appears in many of Canada's major newspapers. Dr. Seiden is the author of Chapter 4, "Frankly, Doctor...: Your Health During Retirement". The medical views expressed in this chapter are those of the author.

# INDEX

# ADDENDUM

**IMPORTANT UPDATE FOR QUEBEC RESIDENTS**

After PLANNING YOUR RETIREMENT went to press, the Quebec government introduced a budget which alters some of the tax and estate planning information given in chapters five and six.

The most important of these changes are:

1. As of midnight April 23rd, 1985, *succession duties* and *gift taxes* in the province of Quebec were abolished.

2. *Quebec Stock Savings Plan (QSSP)*

   (a) Starting in 1986, the maximum allowable annual tax deduction for buying stocks in blue chip companies (assets exceed $1 billion) under the QSSP will be $1,000.

   (b) Also, as of 1986, the total deductible limit for QSSP stocks will be reduced from $20,000 to $10,000.

   (c) The rate of deduction eligible for shares in smaller companies will also be scaled down, as follows:

   | 1985 | 1986 and later |
   |------|----------------|
   | 150% | 100% |
   | 100% | 75% |
   | 50% | 50% |

3. Starting in 1986, taxpayers claiming more than $20,000 in tax-sheltered expenditures will be limited to a maximum of 40% of their net income. In effect, this imposes a minimum income tax upon high-income earners.

4. Starting in January 1986 there will be a major reorganization of the personal income tax structure related to deductions and exemptions.

5. As of midnight April 23rd, 1985 the 9% sales tax will apply to premiums on *all* types of insurance with the exception of that portion of any life insurance premium representing savings.

For more detailed information, consult your broker, accountant, notary or lawyer; or you can request a copy of the budget by writing to:

Ministère du revenu du Québec
3 Complexe Desjardins
C.P. 3000
Succursales Desjardins
Montréal, Québec
H5B 1A4